SHARKS

of STEEL

Yogi Kaufman and Paul Stillwell

Photography by Steve and Yogi Kaufman

Developed in association with Lance K. Shultz, Auburn Productions, Inc., East Liverpool, Ohio.

NAVAL INSTITUTE PRESS
Annapolis, Maryland

LIBRARY OF CONGRESS CATALOGING-IN-PUBLICATION DATA
Kaufman, Yogi.
    Sharks of steel / Robert Y. "Yogi" Kaufman and Paul
    Stillwell ; photography by Steve and Yogi Kaufman.
        p. cm.
    ISBN 1-55750-451-2 (acid-free)
    1. Submarine boats.   I. Stillwell, Paul, 1944–   II. Title.
    V857.K28   1992
    359.3'257–dc20   92-35231

Printed in the United States of America on acid-free paper ∞

9 8 7 6 5 4 3 2
First printing

PAGE i: USS *Salt Lake City*, high-speed surface run.
PAGE ii-iii: USS *Sunfish* (l) and *Hammerhead*, Norfolk,
        Virginia, sunset.
PAGE iv-v: USS *Will Rogers* departs for patrol from
        Holy Loch, Scotland.
TITLE PAGE: Trident sub, USS *Georgia* dives on trials in
        Dabob Bay, Washington.
LEFT: USS *Jefferson City* off Norfolk, Virginia.

Mako

Young
Warriors

Contents

Boomers

The Stealth of Silence

Preface

Early in the twentieth century, several technological innovations began to change the manner in which men went about the unpleasant business of waging war. As machine guns came into use in the great land armies, juggernauts of steel were invented to counter their withering fire, and in time juggernaut was to face juggernaut rather than bayonet battling bayonet. There were soon to be aircraft, at first designed to drop bombs on and to strafe hapless troops, but finally to shoot down other airplanes.

So it was on the surface of the oceans. Big ships of heavy steel armor and big guns, or small, fast ships designed to be the greyhounds of the seas, each countered foes of similar character in a grand scheme to keep the sea-lanes open and to influence the war on land. But in World War I a new player arrived—the U-boat. This tiny, malodorous contraption was to engage in a sort of warfare that was in no way considered gentlemanly or fair. The whole U-boat war embodied stealth and surprise, a guerrilla action more in keeping with Mosby's Raiders of Civil War fame, or even of a vast pod of sharks feeding on helpless victims. Proper warriors of classic upbringing might be outraged at the entire U-boat campaign—it smacked of piracy and was, by Jove, illegal! But it worked,

◄

During World War I the word "U-boat" entered the world's lexicon, a contraction of the German *Unterseeboot.* And the U-boat entered the world's consciousness as well because of its ability to devastate the commercial shipping of the Allied Powers. The sinking of the British passenger liner *Lusitania* in 1915 had an electric effect on world opinion and compelled the Germans to suspend their practice of unrestricted submarine warfare. When the strategic situation led the Germans to restore such operations in 1917, the United States entered the global conflict. Here, German artist Klaus Bergen has captured the atmosphere on board *U-53;* her crewmen wear oilskins to protect themselves from the Atlantic spray. *(Naval Historical Center, NH 88401-KN)*

almost bringing Britain to its knees. Wonderful paintings depict the tough breed of sailor who manned those small coffins, who was shielded in oilskins against the mountainous seas that broke over the bridges. Those men sank twenty million tons of shipping—a fleet of ships that, stretched bow to stern, would reach some four hundred miles. Though submariners were considered unkempt barbarians, they sounded a loud wake-up call for chivalry! They would find use again.

World War II, of course, provided the real proving ground for submarines in naval warfare and indelibly impressed naval officers with the importance of knowing how to fight beneath the surface. Again, the impetus came from the U-boats. They destroyed more than 2,600 merchant ships, despite having started the war with only 56 good boats. The Germans built a tremendous submarine force during the war, most of which was sunk, but the U-boats sank an average of 3.4 targets each. The records of such U-boat "aces" as Otto Kretschmer, Wolfgang Lüth, Günther Prien, and Reinhard Hardegen are legend.

Just as legendary were the exploits of the submariners of other combatant navies. British skippers of renown—Miers, Wanklyn, Plaice, Donald Cameron, and Tubby Linton, among others—earned their nation's highest award for valor, the Victoria Cross, and the top Russian "ace" of the war, the man who sank the most targets, was Aleksey Matiyasevich.

U.S. submarines, although starting with a considerably less well defined rationale than the Germans', and with a deplorable state of weapon development, nonetheless sank 1,178 merchant ships and added no fewer than 214 Japanese naval ships. Of the total of 288 subs that saw action, 52 were lost, and with them some of the most heroic of wartime crews and skippers. Names such as Dick O'Kane, Eugene Fluckey, George Street, Dudley "Mush" Morton, Slade Cutter, Lawson "Red" Ramage, and Sam Dealey head the list of highly successful skippers.

The industrial capacity of the United States, of course, was the driving force in determining the outcome of the war. In 1945 no fewer than thirty-nine submarines were completed at seven building yards. In the previous year sixty-eight were commissioned, with an astounding twenty-six constructed at Electric Boat Company alone! (The United States in the recent past has commissioned perhaps half a dozen submarines in a good year.)

It is with this backdrop that this book is offered, with no wish to ignore the accomplishments of any group, nor to play heavily upon the heroics of any individual. The hero, should there have to be one, is the ordinary submariner who has chosen to man these strange vehicles—old or new, of whatever nation—and those members of his family who have had to live with his long absences and with his silence when asked about his business.

This book presents a number of unusual historical photographs. One can feel the crowded conditions, the wet bridges, and the condensate-laden compartments, all of which were a daily part of submarine life in "the old days." Then, in words and vivid color photographs, comes an insider's view of just what life is like on modern submarines, which are true marvels of technology. The reader will move from the patrol of a diesel submarine in World War II, to the stealthy operations of a modern nuclear attack sub, to the secretiveness of a ballistic-missile submarine, and finally to a glimpse of the largest of all submarines, the Russian Typhoon.

Neat rows of onlookers, both on the deck of the U-boat and on the dock above, watch as Grand Admiral Karl Dönitz presents the Knight Cross to the submarine's skipper. The scene captured by artist Klaus Bergen depicts the man who was responsible for both the great success and the great failure of Germany's World War II submarine force. Guided by Dönitz's genius, the U-boats operated almost untrammeled in the early part of the war, inflicting horrific losses on Allied merchantmen. But his procedures proved the U-boats' undoing, for he relied on the heavy use of radio transmissions. Allied code breakers were thus able to predict with a good deal of assurance where the U-boats would be. Lying in wait for the Germans would be antisubmarine ships and aircraft. By mid-1943 the German submarine effort peaked and began a downhill slide. From then to the end of the war, the iron coffins carried their crews to undersea graves in ever-increasing numbers. When the losses were finally calculated, nine of every ten German submariners had perished. *(Naval Historical Center, NH 85950-KN)* ▶

To this scene from around 1940, Klaus Bergen has affixed the optimistic title "Going to England." It's the sort of image that one would expect on a recruiting poster as Germany's combat arms head off to face the enemy—a Type VII U-boat, equipped with a net cutter, and a phalanx of Ju-88 bombers overhead. Both bombers and submarines inflicted enormous damage on Great Britain in 1940, but Adolf Hitler never mustered the courage for the knockout blow. His projected invasion of the British Isles, Operation Sea Lion, never came off. The English Channel, narrow though it is, was too formidable an obstacle. *(Naval Historical Center, NH 88403-KN)* ▶

◄ Perhaps the most dedicated of all U.S. submarine commanding officers during World War II was Dick O'Kane, here depicted by the noted portrait artist Albert K. Murray. Besides his success in sinking ships, O'Kane earned the gratitude of the many downed aviators that his boat, *Tang*, rescued on lifeguard missions. O'Kane was indisputably at the top, credited after the war with twenty-four sinkings and nearly ninety-four thousand tons of Japanese shipping. At that, his achievement might have been even greater but for a malfunctioning torpedo that left *Tang*, made a circular run, and came back to sink the boat that fired it. O'Kane was one of a handful of men to escape from *Tang* after she sank to the bottom; the few survivors spent the rest of the war as Japanese prisoners. O'Kane has told the story of *Tang* in a memoir titled *Clear the Bridge*, and he has written a second book about his service in *Wahoo* under another top skipper, Dudley "Mush" Morton. *(Navy Combat Art Collection)*

◄ The crew on board U-858 is American because she has just been surrendered by the Germans at war's end in May 1945. The officer in charge of the boarding party, standing with a megaphone on the Bridge, is Lieutenant Commander Willard D. Michael. As the Type IXC U-boat approaches Cape Henlopen, Delaware, her overhead escort includes a Navy blimp and one of the earliest military helicopters in service, a Sikorsky HNS-1. *(National Archives, 80-H-K-3319A)*

In the real world of submarines, there really is not a USS *Mako*, an attack boat named *Brooklyn*, or a Trident submarine named *Hawaii*—not that there shouldn't be, and there could very well be at some time in the future. For some obscure reason, the Navy saw fit to name submarines for fish and even slugs with far less fighting attributes than that game shark, the Mako, even resorting to "Trembler" at one point during World War II! Fortunately, wiser heads noted a disconnect between the names and the message the names were supposed to convey, and Trembler became *Quillback*, an improvement to be sure, but still somewhat lacking the ring of *Seawolf*, *Hammerhead*, or *Seadragon*.

Mako, *Brooklyn*, and *Hawaii* represent the wonderful ships of their periods. The actions depicted are typical and have occurred dozens or even hundreds of times. The submarine crewmen described, while fictitious, do in fact resemble sailors who man or manned submarines; although the resemblances are not purely coincidental, they may easily fit dozens of submarine veterans. It is hoped that a glimmer of submarine life will emerge, and that the reader will appreciate some of the challenges of living in these "sharks of steel."

The World War II submariners provided the springboard from which has exploded the magnificent submarine forces of the United States, Russia, the United Kingdom, and France. Our captains and crew members today benefit from a process that has melded the best of U-boat experience and doctrine from two wars, and of Allied wolf pack and independent submarine exploits from World War II, with the labor and anguish of the hundreds of "diesel sailors," shipbuilders, inventors, industrialists, and naval leaders who have accomplished the transition to the modern nuclear navies. No single person can claim full credit, although some individuals like Hyman Rickover have been major contributors, but all past submariners have helped to shape their modern counterparts, who are smart, bright, highly trained, serious, and skilled in the technologies of their trade. May the mathematics that they have mastered work out in their future formulas, to wit, that the number of their surfacings equals the number of their dives!

This unusual view of a World War II Fleet submarine shows USS *Perch*, a diesel boat. Prominent are the engine exhausts, the teak deck, the heavy propeller guards on the stern, the bridge and conning tower structure, the lookout platforms, and a feature not seen in modern subs—a flag hoist. *(U.S. Navy)* ► ►

◀◀ *(Inset)*

This is among the thousands of images produced by a superb team of photographers assembled by Edward Steichen to document the Navy's role in World War II. In the summer of 1943 Steichen and several members of his team went to New London and Groton, Connecticut, home of the submarine school, submarine base, and one of the nation's top shipyards, Electric Boat Company. The skill of Steichen's crew is evident in this view, for the photographer has chosen an angle that gives one the feeling of being in the belly of a whale. The circular frames define the size and shape that the hull of the submarine *Blenny* will achieve. These skeletal forgings are coated with zinc chromate, a preservative to protect against rust, before they are painted. On 9 April 1944, nearly a year after the picture was taken, *Blenny* was christened by Florence King, daughter of Admiral Ernest J. King, a former submariner who was then serving as Chief of Naval Operations. *(National Archives, 80-GK-15064)*

◀ *(Inset)*

All was pageantry, color, pomp, and circumstance as the fleet boat *Swordfish* awaited her launching at the Mare Island Navy Yard on 22 July 1939. The yard at Vallejo, California, was important for submarines during World War II, both for constructing new boats and for repairing and modernizing boats coming back from patrols. The first submarine built at Mare Island was *V-6*, later *Nautilus*, which was commissioned in 1930. That boat's career ended in June 1945 when—in imitation of the normal christening ceremony—someone smashed a bottle of champagne over her forward 6-inch gun and decommissioned her. *Swordfish* did not have such a peaceful ending. In January 1945 she was lost between Okinawa and Japan during her unlucky thirteenth war patrol. *(National Archives, 80-GK-13791)*

Although one seldom associates the green hills of Scotland with U.S. submarine operations in World War II, the base at Roseneath did indeed provide a haven for the six modern fleet boats of Submarine Squadron 50 and their aged tender *Beaver.* Combat artist Dwight Shepler has painted three of the six in "Jerry Hunters." Ordered to Scotland as a political gesture by President Franklin D. Roosevelt, the submarines made twenty-seven war patrols, including one in support of the North Africa landings in November 1942. As Clay Blair, Jr., recounted in his monumental book *Silent Victory,* the executive officer of one of the six boats, R. E. M. Ward of *Gurnard,* seemed to have an uncanny talent. The boat's skipper, Herb Andrews, explained, "Ward was amazing. He always seemed to know ahead of time what I wanted to talk about and had prepared himself thoroughly. Then I found out why: he'd peep in and take a look at my calendar, on which I jotted down items for future discussion." *(Navy Combat Art Collection)* ▶

Acknowledgments

Our too few words of thanks offered here only begin to express our appreciation for the help provided us in our search for archival photography and in our creation of the lively images of submariners today.

In our search for unusual photographs of an era when color photography was only being introduced, we are particularly grateful to Bill Galvani, director of Submarine Force Library and Museum at Groton, Connecticut, who was very helpful in providing photographs and information. Chuck Haberlein and Ed Finney provided access to the fine photographic collection of the Naval Historical Center, as did Dale Conley at the National Archives.

We are in debt to two Chiefs of Naval Operation of the United States Navy, Admirals Frank Kelso and Carl Trost, and to the Director Nuclear Propulsion, Admiral Bruce DeMars, who assisted in providing us access to the United States submarines portrayed in our book. Others whose help and guidance were invaluable were Rear Admiral Kendell Pease, Lieutenant Commanders Dave Morris and Scott Wilson, and Lieutenants Susan Haeg and Bob Ross, who labor constantly in the Navy's public-relations efforts. Every command echelon of the submarine forces provided magnificent assistance to our photographers, who are in the debt of hundreds of submariners—men and women—who demonstrated full measures of patience and cooperation. In particular, the assistance of Rear Admiral Larry Marsh, Captain John Padgett, and two great sub skippers and their crews—Captain Dick Raaz and *Georgia,* and Commander Ed Jablonski and *Topeka*—was especially important to our combination book-television production. We hope that all of you find our product worthy of your sacrifices and performance.

With no attempt to test the flexibility of our printers by using the Cyrillic alphabet, we wish to express to another chief of another great Navy—Fleet Admiral Vladimir N. Chernavin, then Commander in Chief Soviet Navy and Deputy USSR Minister of Defense—our unbounded appreciation for the unusual access provided to Soviet submarine and training activities. While all Navy contacts in Russia were frank, open, and extremely helpful, Rear Admiral Yuriy Fedorov and Captains (2nd Rank) Sergey Kalashnikov and Eduard Abramovich were especially forthcoming. Nazhdarovije!

Finally, while we congratulate the staff of the Naval Institute Press for forbearance and flexibility in completing a new type of effort, we want to single out the efforts of our designer, Pam Schnitter, and editor, Anthony Chiffolo, who successfully submerged his aviator's wings for a short time in producing our account of steel sharks!

Young Warriors

MANNING THE "BOATS"

On any day from 1942 to 1945 a traveler on the railroads between Boston and New York cannot help noticing, during a short stop at New London, Connecticut, the ebb and flow of vigorous young men who are garbed in the blue uniforms long associated with the American sailor—tight bell-bottomed trousers with the traditional thirteen-button flap fly, snug blouses, and dress "flathats" or white sailor's hats. These are the warriors of the day, and this New England town has become the heart of submarine activity and training.

Excited urgency animates those who are boarding the train. For many who are disembarking, a sort of regret prevails, the excesses of big-city liberty evident in their red-eyed stares. The very youngest, somewhat self-conscious youths—those with the undecorated chests—are obviously recruits for the Submarine School across the Thames River. The experienced men display a swaggering pride in the distinctive silver "dolphins" of the "Silent Service" and the rainbow of campaign ribbons or awards on their chests. Young officers who are "qualified" wear a gold version of the dolphin pin on their

◄

The crew of *Dorado* musters projectiles for the boat's deck gun in Georges Schreiber's "Clear for Action." Lookouts on the conning tower and an officer on the deck scan the surroundings with their binoculars. World War II fleet-boat skippers differed in their attitudes about the use of deck guns against small craft. Some figured that any Japanese they encountered were the enemy and thus fair game. Others abhorred the idea of cold-blooded killing of defenseless individuals, no matter what their nationality. The latter shared the view of Bill Post, captain of *Gudgeon* (SS-211) and *Spot* (SS-413). He did not embrace the idea of shooting at the survivors of ships that had been sunk, explaining, "When they were still aboard ship, they were the enemy; once they were in the water, they had become fellow mariners in distress." *(Navy Combat Art Collection, KN-21777)*

uniforms, which are either khaki, grey, or the more traditional Navy blue.

The buzzing chatter of both officers and men touches upon the tattered condition of the wartime "cattle cars" in which they are crowded and the exorbitant though special military price for a round-trip ticket to Washington—a heady $9.35! With little regard for the area's accorded status as the "submarine capital of the United States," some of the submariners direct criticism at the "whistle stop" status of New London, Groton, and Norwich, which are their daily liberty sites: "Not enough bars." "Cops are tough on sailors, but not like Norfolk!" Others laugh uproariously at the foibles of "regulars" at a plethora of Bank Street bars, be it Tiny's Heat Wave ("Where the elite of the fleet meet!"), Ernie's, "The Elbo," or Danny Shea's Yellow Dog Saloon.

Nonregulation, skin-tight, "tailor-made" blouses disclose brilliantly embroidered inner cuffs when upturned during the relaxation of liberty, and the tattoo needle's artistry appears as "Mother," "Love," "Sally and Pete," "Guitarro," or the dolphin emblem. Tax-free "sea stores" cigarettes, bought at the bargain price of seventy cents per carton, soon make their contribution to the already dense fog of heavy smoke in the compartments. A gentleman traveler, far more advanced in years than these submariners and curious about their "silent service," marvels at the energy and confidence they display and smiles at their bluster. Clearly, it's a time for youth and a time for challenge, both in abundance in these excited and expectant young warriors.

During the station stop, a veteran sailor offers a cigarette to the gentleman, who takes the opportunity to ask about the ribbon representing the Silver Star Medal. His question brings a grateful nod and a shy smile, but that is all. The sailor, instead, explains that each bronze star adorning his submarine combat pin represents another patrol awarded a "successful" rating, following the initial award of the pin for his first successful patrol. He looks forward to another good patrol, but this one will be on the new boat to which he has just reported—USS *Mako*. From this exchange, it is very clear to the gentleman what information these Navy men can discuss. People, fine; submarine life, fine; operations, never!

So the gentleman contents himself with asking about the

sailor's motivation for seeking submarine duty, and his friendly probing taps a well of deep feelings. The volunteer has been heart and hallmark of the U.S. submarine force since its beginning. A man has to want to serve in it. However, life in a submarine is not for everyone. Mothers, sisters, sweethearts, and sometimes fathers have questioned the reasoning powers of their young man who contemplates a career in "the boats." Those who are not called cannot easily understand the desire to live deep within the oceans, not even by appealing to their sense of "adventure" or machismo. Most people would agree that living in vessels referred to variously as "sewer pipes," "pigboats," or "steel coffins" doesn't quite smack of normalcy—but not a submariner. The gentleman concludes that there is a special satisfaction in facing challenging jobs, like operating a submarine, and mastering them.

A breathless young sailor who literally dived for the departing train's platform as it pulled away joins the gentleman. Conversation comes easily, and a few simple questions regarding his insignia, his rate, and his shiny dolphins bring a flood of words. A torpedoman third class, he sports a spanking new "crow" (really an eagle) and a single red chevron that marks his status as the most junior of petty officers. He is proud of his wartime service in submarines and grins warmly as he refers to the "chicken" regulations of the surface ships, which he has avoided. He points out the advantages of an additional 50 percent hazardous-duty pay. It will help to save a nest egg for later education or marriage, but he quickly adds that he would be in submarines without the extra money. The important thing drawing him to subs is the early acceptance as a part of a team—being a "player" and having some importance. Like others around the compartment, he refers to a war patrol as a "run." On his very first run he served as a messcook, the lowest form of life on board, and was responsible for dish washing, spud peeling, and head cleaning, but he had also been placed on lookout and planesman watches. On his second run, he became a battle-stations stern planesman, literally controlling the boat at the most important times. Now, with his new dolphins, he's assigned to a new-construction boat—USS *Mako*—being completed at Electric Boat Company in Groton—known throughout the submarine world as EB. He can't wait to get back to the Pacific war in his "new, seven-million-dollar home."

The gentleman makes his way to the club car. An empty spot at a table puts him next to a salty character, whose gold hash marks and insignia of twelve years of service and good conduct show just a bit of patina from the sea air. The gentleman's offer of a drink brings a nod of acceptance, and then a scowl from each as they remark the wartime bottle of Kinsey's, but the shared disappointment breaks the ice. The submariner is a chief motor machinist's mate, referred to as a "motor mac," and he has been a leading "auxiliaryman," one of those who

oversee most of the submarine's systems—air, hydraulic, air-conditioning and refrigeration, pumps—that keep the sub running but aren't specifically torpedo, engine room, or electrically related. He explains that he completed five runs on his last boat and was recently assigned as a leading instructor at Submarine School, but now he has been "ripped out" to be the chief auxiliaryman of a new boat—USS *Mako*.

When queried, he describes a long dissatisfaction with the "spit and polish" battleship Navy—the weekly inspections, the endless hours with no sleep at battle stations when no enemy is around. The happiest day of his life was when he reported to a boat after Sub School. He expresses quiet confidence in his own and his shipmates' abilities and great pride in his last skipper, whom he quotes, "Submarines might not win this war, but if you didn't have 'em, you might lose it!" Without giving details he mentions that his sub sank a sizable number of ships. He enjoyed the closeness of that crew, the frequent beer ball games at the between-patrols "rest camp" on Guam—with officers and chiefs against the "white hats"—and the hours spent, over beers of course, simply watching the gooney birds crash clumsily into the airplane runways. Though he expresses the wish, heard often on this train, for a quick and successful end to the war, he also acknowledges that the Navy was his life before the war and will continue to be for a twenty- or thirty-year career—so long as it's "in the boats."

A young officer in sharply pressed, gabardine khakis enters the car and, on noting an empty spot, asks to join the table. The shiny gold braid of the star and single stripe on his shoulder boards have yet to get the tarnish of the sea. Just one month out of the U.S. Naval Academy, he's just starting Submarine School, a four-month stint, after which he'll get orders to a sub. Flushed with the prosperity of his ensign pay, $150 per month—riches when compared with his $12 midshipman's stipend—he offers to buy drinks and enters the conversation. He had been completely unimpressed with life on board the old battleships *Arkansas* and *New York* on midshipman cruises, and a knowing smile passes between the chief and the gentleman traveler. The ensign speaks with enthusiasm about Commander Slade Cutter's accounts of his submarine patrols. One of the Navy's top skippers of the war, Cutter was enthusiastic and colorful. His talk highlighted the fantastic success of submarines and sold the ensign and many of his classmates, one hundred of whom entered Submarine School. Expecting to be an important player shortly after Sub School, the ensign looks for confirmation to the chief, who adds that he will have plenty to keep him busy—studying for his qualification, standing officer-of-the-deck and diving-officer watches, working as a department head, and squeezing in three or four hours of sleep a day. (Neither could know at the time that the ensign would be ordered to USS *Mako*.)

Leaving the train in New York, the gentleman reflects on

how little he has actually learned about the lives led by the young sailors as they fight their battles on top of and beneath the oceans. But the time spent in their company has lightened his step and brightened his day. He recalls a photograph passed between several friends—an image of bushy-bearded, grinning men who looked more like buccaneers than Navy sailors. Why the broom tied to the top of the periscope? A youngster had chortled, "Clean sweep! We sank four ships and had a successful patrol!"

In a few weeks these eager young men and some seventy others will come together to form a crew, specifically, the crew of USS *Mako*. Novice will join veteran in actions that can spell life or death. They will form boarding parties, armed with submachine guns, and pour over the gunwales of damaged enemy ships; will land reconnaissance details in rubber boats or send swimmers ashore with lines to rescue observation "beach watchers"; will respond to the call, "Battle Stations, Gun Action," spilling from the hatches as soon as the boat has leaped like a cork out of the water, to cover the enemy with a hailstorm of 5-inch, 40-millimeter, 20-millimeter, and .50-caliber machine-gun fire; and will, from the hidden depths, launch torpedoes to destroy the vitals of enemy ships. A hazardous but heady concoction, indeed!

These young men will also dive away from the tracer fire or bombs of attacking aircraft and flee from the depth charges that can shake their boat apart. And when the enemy's weapons find her, her novices will quickly become veterans, fighting to control the spray from ruptured piping, to catch their breath amidst the acrid smoke from burning panels or motors, to overcome their fear and save their boat.

A bonding experience? Believe it!

As World War II came to an end and security restrictions were eased, Electric Boat Company, understandably proud of the record compiled by its products, published a colorful painting to show off its handiwork. The result lets us look at the various compartments in which crew members lived and worked. Much of the success of the fleet boat belonged to an engineering genius named Andrew I. McKee, a Naval Academy graduate who specialized in naval construction. To the science of submarine design, he brought a good deal of art as well; the submarine improvements he wrought were inspired. *(Electric Boat Company, courtesy Submarine Force Library and Museum)*

▲

The gooney birds on Midway have seen it all, including the use of the island as an advanced base for U.S. submarines in World War II. It was a place where boats could refuel, get repair work done, and give their crews some rest and relaxation between patrols. To be sure, it was no Hawaii, but it had the strategic advantage of being closer to the patrol areas, thus cutting down on transit time. In artist Paul Sample's "Departure," USS *Trigger*, commanded by Lieutenant Commander Roy Benson, is setting out on patrol. The boat compiled a fine record under Benson and his successor, Dusty Dornin. They were aided no little by their outstanding executive officer, Ned Beach, who recorded the boat's story in the book *Submarine*. *Trigger*'s illustrious career ended when she was lost in March 1945 during her twelfth war patrol. Her final skipper was Commander Dave Connole. Afterward, Mrs. Connole sought Benson's help in securing the widow's benefits to which she was entitled. Benson, a lifelong bachelor until then, gave her the help she needed and married her in the bargain. *(Naval Historical Center, NH 94736-KN)*

At the very top of a fleet boat were the periscopes, tapered so that as little as possible could be spotted by an enemy. This Steichen shot makes a hero of the lookout in the periscope shears, and rightfully so. Despite the electronic sensors of the fleet boats, the lookouts played indispensable roles, both offensively and defensively. The human eye is capable of spotting both targets and threats not discernible by other means. When boats were operating on the surface, lookouts scanned the horizon and sky, searching particularly for aircraft because planes could swoop down and deliver an attack the most quickly and thus with the greatest surprise. At the beginning of World War II a one-lookout watch was standard, but that was soon beefed up to four so that someone would be scanning all four quadrants of the sky and sea simultaneously. Submarine crews were enlarged to provide for the increased number of lookouts. This man is wearing the standard shipboard enlisted uniform of World War II, dungarees, and from his belt hangs the collection of keys that was also a sailor's trademark. *(National Archives, 80-GK-16060)*

▶

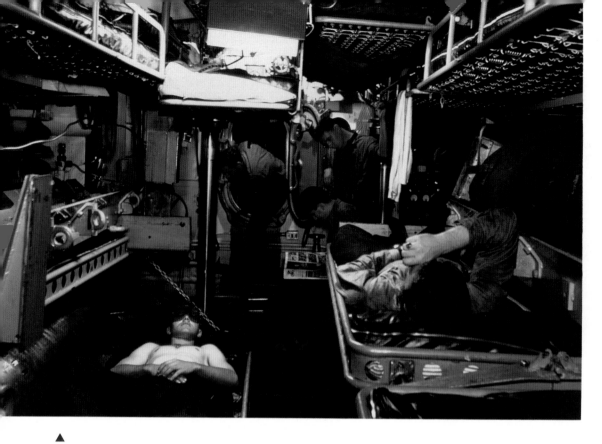

▲

A ceremony is held to ▶ award the "silver dolphins" to a qualified submariner, a petty officer aboard USS *Tautog*. Part of *Tautog*'s ritual is the reading of an excerpt from the patrol diary of the original World War II *Tautog*, a ship with a fantastic record of success. The readings, from that day years ago that corresponds to the date of this ceremony, can vary widely: on some days a ship was sunk; on others, the *Tautog* herself suffered a near calamity.

As the Steichen crew moved inside a fleet boat, it found the sort of claustrophobic conditions that have made submarine duty a volunteer-only proposition. Bunks are stacked into the berthing compartment wherever room is available. In the center an enlisted man hunches over to pass through an access hatch from the next compartment, taking care to lift his leg over the "knee-knocker" coaming. Nearby, two men scan a picture magazine. In the lower left, a white-chested sailor wears goggles and stretches out for a submariner's version of a sunbath. The man at right shields his eyes from the ultraviolet light while trying to take a nap. To an outsider, it all looks cramped and unnatural; to a submariner, it looks like home. *(National Archives, 80-GK-16125)*

Nuclear-power-school students at Orlando, Florida, familiarize themselves with the details of motors and turbine generators. ▶

During the Steichen team's visit to New London in 1943, one of the photographers stopped by the submarine school to record a classic tableau: a chief petty officer passing out the skinny to a new crop of future submariners while two other chiefs await their turns. On the bulkhead are diagrams of the type of boat in which the men will be serving. All pore over their notes except the young gent in the foreground, unable to stifle a yawn. What became of these young men of 1943? How many survived the war? How many became chief petty officers themselves? *(National Archives, 80-G-K-16120)* ▶▶

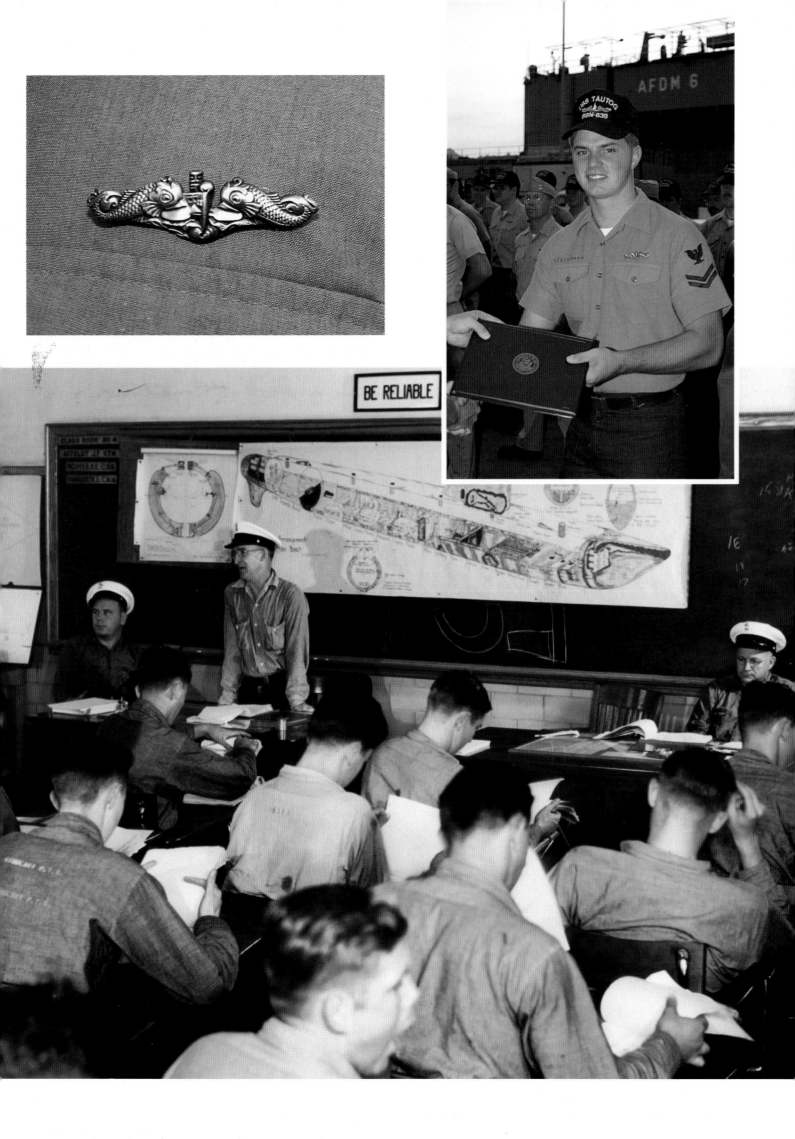

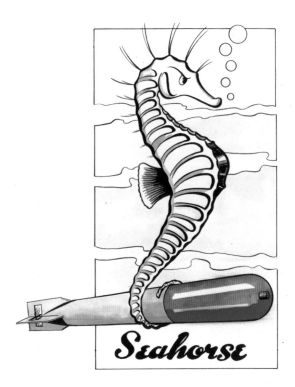

Slade Cutter, shown here as a captain in 1952, established a superb record as commanding officer of the fleet boat *Seahorse* in 1943 and 1944. He was credited with sinking nineteen enemy ships comprising a total of seventy-two thousand tons. Although sources differ on the scores achieved by other submarine captains, Cutter was certainly in the top five, possibly as high as second among all U.S. skippers in terms of ships sunk. He was aggressive without being foolhardy—that aggressiveness having been demonstrated a decade earlier when he was a topflight football player and boxer at the Naval Academy. His professional ability combined with luck—an almost uncanny ability to sniff out Japanese ships—to produce impressive results. Slade Cutter was a leader, an officer who served as an example throughout the submarine force for his skill and courage. *(National Archives, 80-GK-13287; Disney Studio, courtesy Navy Combat Art Collection)*

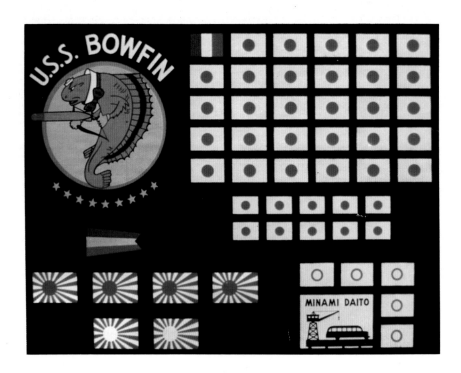

◄ Colorful "Battle Flag" of USS *Bowfin* (SS-287), one of the more successful submarines of the Pacific war. Miniature Japanese flags depict ship sinkings, the "rising suns" on the left representing warships, while merchantmen are shown by the sunballs on the right. Why the pier and bus? In August 1944 LCDR John Corbus took the sub in very close to a harbor of a small island, attacking a ship at anchor with three torpedoes, and another moored at the pier with another salvo. He had noted on the pier the bus taking sailors from the ship to a picnic, just before the torpedoes struck. *Bowfin*'s claim—"Two ships, one quay, one bus."

Sea Dog

Lamprey

Plaice

Barb

During World War II, when patriotism was a salable commodity in the movie theaters, the Walt Disney studio was also giving it away. The artists in the famous cartoon factory generously drew dozens of designs as insignias for ships, aircraft squadrons, and other military units. Included was a series honoring various submarines. In some cases the design is a play on the boat's name, as in *Sea Dog*; in others, the artist attempted to depict what the real sea creature looked like while drawing a design for its namesake; and for such obscure fish as the plaice, a little imagination spruced up the image by throwing in Jiminy Cricket, a character from the feature-length cartoon *Pinocchio*, which had been released shortly before the war began. *(Disney Studio, courtesy Navy Combat Art Collection)*

Queenfish

Mako

FIGHTING THE PACIFIC WAR

he shark is hungry.

It moves slowly, stealthily, using its taste, smell, sight, even the touch of its skin to sense any indication, however slight, that prey might be near. For prey is raison d'être to the shark—the very justification for its existence. The ultimate killing machine, it has a marvelous system of reactive nerves that can instantly trigger a slashing, frenzied attack so rapid its prey has no warning—only a swift and merciful end.

It is June 1944, and another predator searches the ocean. She, too, has sensors, speed, stealth, and a proclivity for prey. *Mako* is the name of this killer, called after a slasher of the deep so combative that it long has been the only shark accorded a ranking as a game fish. Built to resemble her namesake as closely as current technology permits, *Mako* is indeed a shark, though without the cartilage, muscle, teeth, or sandpaper skin of her living counterpart. *Mako* is a shark of steel!

A full eight days have passed since her last real action, but the Japanese have adopted a tactic that keeps the crew's adrenaline flowing. Each afternoon, at almost the same time, a bomber—known among the Allies as a "Betty"—flies out from a nearby island in an apparently random patrol pattern. At some point, always different, the plane drops a large, noisy bomb. Once or twice the concussion has been close enough to

◀

The tattooed sailor is in touch with two vestiges of the submarine's heritage as a submersible torpedo boat: her 5-inch deck gun and her teak deck planking. The old torpedo boats were expected to be able to fight it out on the surface if necessary, using the deck guns. That meant sending gun crews up through the conning tower hatch and out on deck. The teak deck gave more secure footing than a metal hull, still wet from surfacing, would have provided. The gun, with its breech mechanism in the foreground, was an old-timer, essentially the same type used to arm merchant ships against U-boat attack since World War I. *(National Archives, 80-GK-15623)*

cause a few nervous eye rolls, or a tenuous half smile. A new man, making his first patrol, asks, "Are we leaking something that's giving us away?"

A veteran of six patrols replies, "Hell, that's not even close enough to rattle the dishes." But it sure raises the pucker factor.

If the explosion is close enough to give the boat a good shaking, the captain or sometimes the second in command, the executive officer—the "exec"—might walk through the boat, passing some time with the men in each compartment, or having a cup of coffee with the watch in the engine rooms or the torpedo rooms. They would do the same during a very rough storm. It is the captain's way of taking the pulse of the crew.

On this day the captain sits for some minutes in Maneuvering, talking with the electricians who control the motors that drive the propellers. The After Torpedo Room watch sits on the coaming of the open watertight door, tuned in to the "old man," as the captain is known behind his back. Conversation comes easily; USS *Mako* is what submariners call a "very close boat."

Watch standers smile with their captain as they recall the details of their last attack, pride in their success evident in their voices. It was classic submarine business.

Radar had detected two medium tankers moving south along the islands under cover of darkness, just inside the 10-fathom curve. They were lightly escorted by one old destroyer and a shallow-draft *Chidori*-class antisubmarine ship. Because only a few short hours of darkness remained by then, a flank speed "end around" was called for—*Mako* would run parallel to the enemy, attempting to race in front of the group and dive for attack just before sunrise. To complicate this maneuver, the submarine had to remain distant enough to avoid detection, which would have sent the quarry scurrying away and the escorts hurrying to attack.

Fortunately, the tankers were slow, and *Mako* was able to gain a position well in front of the group just after it passed the friendly 100-fathom curve. Now there was lots of diving water. From the Conning Tower, the captain passed the word up the hatch, "Take her down, Mike!" The officer of the deck acknowledged with a bellowed, "Clear the Bridge! Clear the

Bridge!" Immediately, the diving alarm sounded—"Ah-oooo-gah! Ah-oooo-gah!"—and then came the words "Dive! Dive!"

To call what occurred next an orchestrated ballet might be appropriate from the standpoint of precision, but not of beauty. Lookouts scrambled from atop the A-frames above the Bridge, legs akimbo, hands sliding over familiar rails. They crashed through the 26-inch hatch into the Conning Tower, thence down another ladder and through another hatch to take station on the wheels that operate the diving planes. Broken limbs or sprained ankles were rare, no doubt because of the frequency of diving practice, unfondly termed by the lookouts as the "bust-your-ass drill."

The chief of the watch was a blur of motion. The levers he pulled opened valves that vented the main ballast tanks, which spilled air into the atmosphere. He was, in essence, deliberately sinking *Mako*. Next he pulled a lever that sealed the "main induction," a 36-inch hole that provided air for the sub and her engines.

At that moment the Bridge hatch slammed shut and was dogged down by the quartermaster. The officer of the deck shouted, "Last man down! Hatch secured!" To take charge of the dive, he continued down to Control, where the chief of the watch was testing the boat for airtightness. The hiss of high-pressure air was deafening.

In every compartment sailors "buttoned up" to withstand the pressures of the sea. Electricians in Maneuvering smoothly tripped out the diesel engines and slammed levers forward and back. They were shifting the power source for the main motors, which drive the sub's propellers, from the diesels to the main storage battery. In a blur of motion often likened to apes' swinging on a trapeze, motor machinist's mates in the engine rooms kicked and pulled levers and spun valves, sealing off the piping that carried diesel exhaust and air for the engines.

So noisy and furious was the action that the diving party used hand signals to buttress the orders given by voice. Strict adherence to standard phraseology was mandatory. Men said "shut," not "close"—"close" sounds too much like "blow," which might pop the boat to the surface in front of a destroyer or aircraft.

As *Mako* leveled off at periscope depth, the announcement, "Battle Stations, Torpedo" rang through the boat, followed by the gonging of the General Alarm. By this time all hands, even those who had been able to sleep during the high-speed end around, were wide-eyed and alert as they manned their stations. Terse orders crackled across the phone circuits, repeated or acknowledged by experienced men who wore the reliable sound-powered headsets. Men skilled in damage control were stationed in each compartment. In the torpedo rooms, torpedoman's mates flooded the torpedo tubes, and extra men prepared to reload the torpedoes once an initial salvo was shot. The "first team" was in place, and *Mako* was ready to attack.

The long end around had placed the sub on the "base course" of the target group, the average direction traveled by the enemy ships as they zigzagged to confuse an attacker. The radar had accurately tracked their course and speed. With this information, the torpedo-data computer, or TDC, required only the smallest of corrections as the submarine jockeyed in response to each zigzag made by the targets. The TDC's output, the gyro angle, would enable the torpedoes to follow a collision course directly to their prey. Jerry, the torpedo officer and TDC operator, enjoys a reputation as a skilled craftsman, but the tracking had been so accurate that he pronounced the run "duck soup," signaling that his skills were superfluous this time, and made only the tiniest adjustments. Some of the men in the fire-control party plotted the bearings and marked the ranges called out after each look with the periscope. By measuring the distance run against the time, they too solved for the enemy's course and speed, as a check on the TDC.

The radiomen, who upon diving become sonar operators, reported "turn counts," the number of beats per minute of the enemy ships' propellers, from which speed could be determined and checked against the TDC solution. Other watch standers plotted the tracks of the destroyer and the *Chidori*, which held the captain's attention as the range closed. With each zig of the targets, the captain ordered a new course and speed to intercept. At the low target speed of 8 knots, *Mako*'s task was easy. The screening escorts seemed the only problem, although there had been no indication that *Mako* was detected as they drew near.

Finally, when the submarine began to pass through the screen, one sonar operator was ordered to track the destroyer continuously, another the *Chidori*. The nearest escort was then 2,000 yards away—only a mile. Sonar reported, "*Chidori* turning toward and speeding up!" The Conning Tower became hushed. Then, "*Chidori* pinging—still long scale." Everyone breathed easy: long scale meant that the escort's sonar was still in the search mode; short scale was used to gain steady echo information once a contact was detected.

The skipper barked, "Six-six feet," and the diving officer sent the sub gliding down to 66 feet. At this depth only a foot of periscope would be exposed above the water when the captain sneaked a quick peek to verify the sonar report.

"*Chidori*—bearing—mark" gave her location to the plotters; the TDC was tracking the lead target just beyond.

"*Chidori* has zigged, but he's continuing his swing—angle on the bow thirty starboard and increasing." Because of this maneuver of the screen, *Mako* gained an unobstructed approach to the main targets, unless the *Chidori* swung back.

A two-second peek brought a smile from the captain—"Attababy! He's going by." Then he ordered, "Six-four feet."

One of the advantages of artistic license is the ability to exaggerate for emphasis. Thus the two torpedoes at left in Georges Schreiber's "All Hands Below" appear to be gigantic. Even so, the men of *Dorado* have learned to ignore them and assume as much normality as possible in a decidedly abnormal situation. Given the unavoidable absence of women, an alternative for relaxing is a friendly game of cards with the fellows. Card playing was so popular that special cards were developed for submarine use. When sailors played at night, their berthing compartment would be bathed in red light, rather than white, because red light doesn't diminish night vision. The card players had to be prepared to go topside for watch or battle stations—without having to wait for their pupils to enlarge to accommodate the surrounding darkness. Since red type doesn't show up under red light, the red symbols on each card were outlined in black so that a player could tell what he had in his hand. *(Navy Combat Art Collection, KN-9152; Submarine Force Library and Museum)*

◀

Top If the cooks were crowded, the men eating their concoctions were even more so. These six sailors are indeed finding elbowroom scarce. The dining space also serves other purposes between meals. At right is a bookcase for part of the ship's library. Little wonder that paperback books and miniature editions of national magazines achieved so much popularity with servicemen during World War II. They could fit into lockers and dungaree pockets while the hard-cover books such as these stayed on the shelf. All the way to the left is another aspect of the crew's recreational facilities, a shelf holding phonograph records, including the rumba number with the pink cover. Cassettes and compact-disc players were still considerably in the future; the old-fashioned phonograph was still a necessity for the records of the day. And, by the way, please pass that silver pitcher of milk when you're finished with it. *(National Archives, 80-GK-16022)*

▲

Mail is ever popular on board Navy ships, almost always a cause for taking a break, unless one gets no letters and has to think instead of the imaginary women in the pinups on the bulkhead. "News from Home" is Georges Schreiber's depiction of mail call on board *Dorado* in 1943. Because of the boat's fate a few months hence, there were probably not many more letters after this one. As for the pinups of scantily clad lovelies, they appeared back then in such magazines as *Esquire*, which was about as racy as things got in those days a decade before the advent of *Playboy*. When a man had to sleep above a torpedo and contemplate his mortality daily, it didn't hurt to dream. *(Navy Combat Art Collection, KN-21777)*

◀ Cooks on board submarines acquired a reputation for their skill at turning out delicious meals, and particularly for their ability to do so in cramped quarters. These men are preparing steaks and gravy. As compensation for the hardships of undersea duty, submariners ate well during World War II. While the folks back home had to keep careful track of ration points for such items as meat and sugar, provisions were readily available for submariners. Food was prepared to fit into the limited storage space; for example, chicken was de-boned before being sent to a submariner's freezer. Since there were no jogging tracks or exercise gyms in submarines, the crew members had to watch their diets to ward off weight gain. This picture demonstrates the temptations. *(National Archives, 80-GK-16020)*

In Georges Schreiber's "Up Periscope," one finds a sense of electricity, action, and excitement almost entirely missing in the posed photo from the Steichen team. In 1943, just about the same time the photographers were visiting New London, Schreiber embarked in the newly commissioned *Dorado* and rode her during shakedown to bring an artist's eye to the scene. In this scene of the Conning Tower, as in the Steichen picture, the skipper has his eye to the periscope, but there is much more of a sense that a great deal is happening at once. The man at the periscope is Commander E. C. "Penrod" Schneider, the son of a Navy chief radioman. Schneider was the first and only commanding officer of *Dorado*; she was sunk mistakenly by a U.S. plane in the Atlantic while heading toward Panama in October 1943. She never made it to the Pacific, never made a war patrol. All seventy-six men on board were lost. (*Navy Combat Art Collection, KN-9158*)

▲ When Steichen's crew visited the Control Room of the submarine-school training boat *Marlin* at New London in August 1943, the background was a little too revealing to suit a wartime censor. Notice the dark blotch above the head of the sailor at left, obscuring the deep-depth gauge in between the two dials reporting shallower depths. The large wheels in the hands of the enlisted men are used to control the boat's buoyancy and thus her depth. The skipper at the periscope is Lieutenant Commander John C. Nichols, who survived the sinking of the *Squalus* in 1939 and after the *Marlin* would command the *Silversides* during her last war patrol. The scraped paint on the periscope indicates that it has made many trips up and down as junior officers practiced making approaches against target ships. (*National Archives, 80-G-K-16013*)

At this depth the captain would be able to see over the waves to assure a good attack setup.

The attack itself *was* a ballet. Every motion, every command, was precise, crisp, uncluttered—the result of hours of rehearsal both at sea and in the shore-bound attack teachers, and of numerous actual attacks made during the past year of war.

"Final bearing and shoot! Up scope!" the captain ordered. As the periscope's cross hairs stopped on the target's center, he called, "Bearing, mark."

Jerry cranked the TDC and called, "Set." starting the firing action.

"Shoot!" ordered the assistant TDC operator, who had set the torpedoes to form a "spread" of diverging gyro angles so that they would fan out to ensure a hit.

The chief yeoman, now manning the firing key instead of his customary typewriter, called, "Fire one!" as he depressed the firing key. He fired subsequent torpedoes at eight-second intervals so that earlier-hitting "fish" would not detonate the later ones. *Mako* fired three torpedoes at each tanker.

Each salvo brought in two hits. The shock wave of each torpedo produced a sharp metallic "click" that the submarine felt about a second before the heavy detonation itself. At this short range the blasts gave *Mako* a tremendous shaking, and cheers rang out the length of the boat.

The Japanese escorts roared down the still-visible torpedo wakes toward *Mako,* but she adeptly sought the depths and a friendly concealing thermal layer, one that the enemy sonars couldn't penetrate. "Rig for depth charge!" placed the sub in her most damage-resistant posture, compartment by compartment. She received only a perfunctory going-over, remaining down and opening the range from the carnage she had produced. Only a half dozen depth charges were even reasonably close, and their explosions yielded no broken gauges or spraying water—just enough shaking up to baptize the new crew members into the terror of the war in the Pacific.

As the sounds of the enemy escorts faded, sonar exclaimed, "Breaking up noises and explosions on the bearing of the tankers!" The captain had this report passed on the 1MC announcing system throughout the boat, and the crew responded with upraised thumbs and more cheers.

After that, the men had secured from rig-for-depth-charge and settled down for a much-delayed breakfast and, hopefully, a quiet day to unwind and get a long sleep.

"But, gents, that was last week. We're getting overdue. Thanks for the coffee." And with these words the captain heads for his tiny stateroom to catch what he calls a "preventive nap" against the possibility of a long chase and sleepless night. His routine for the rest of the day would bring "Soup-down"—a light snack of hot soup and sandwiches—as the watch was relieved in the late afternoon, then, after an hour or

so of light reading, he would order *Mako* to surface to charge her batteries. Dinner would bring the usual submarine gourmet delights: steak and—if the supply of stabilized cream, Avocet, held out—homemade ice cream. After dinner—since it's Friday—several hours of cigars and poker for the officers in the Wardroom.

Later that evening *Mako* moves gently in calm seas, the surface so smooth that the swells appear almost oily to the watch standers on the Bridge. A black, black night in the dark of the moon, and the skies are mostly overcast. It's a good night for surface action. Several squalls move toward the submarine from an island some thirty miles distant, the light breezes bringing the pleasant, unmistakable odor of sandalwood, overlaid with faint wisps of fish and seaweed. Lightning sporadically pierces the blackness, illuminating the horizon in the manner of gunfire, each time raising the tension on the Bridge.

On just the last patrol, the "lightning" turned out to be 8-inch projectiles from a Japanese cruiser that patterned themselves uncomfortably close to *Mako*. At that the submarine had engaged all four engines to dash to deeper waters, evading two searching destroyers that appeared by surprise from a concealing rainsquall. Finally, she had been able to pull a comforting hundred-foot blanket of salt water over herself. It had been a poor time for the newly installed marvel, radar, to turn up its toes!

The radar's fine this night. Tuned up by the new radio technician, "Ski," it sweeps the surrounding sea every few minutes. He has comforting proof that the gadget works: rainsqualls show up on the scope in the Conning Tower, though a night shield has changed the presentation from its normal green to a deep ruby color. An enemy ship should produce a strong luminescent pip. Nevertheless, the officer of the deck, or OOD, scans the horizon with binoculars, as do four lookouts and the quartermaster of the watch. Close as *Mako* is to the enemy-held island, the men on the submarine must be constantly alert for any enemy activity, and eyes strain to pick up anything but blackness. They are searching for the white wake of a speeding patrol boat, the "feather" of a nearby periscope, the telltale phosphorescence of sea life caused by a torpedo racing into *Mako*'s vitals—whatever isn't ocean. Fortunately, there has been little enemy air activity at night.

"Keep on the damned ball, Gregory," growls Tex, the quartermaster. "Use your glasses more abaft the beam, and cut out the bull!" He's a taskmaster, driving lookouts hard, but he has superb vision, and no lookout has ever detected a contact at night before him. Tex trains his lookouts relentlessly in search techniques.

The Conning Tower, immediately below the Bridge, is virtually black. A red light shines dimly over the chart desk aft.

A dim red glow along the rim of the compass repeater illuminates the helsman's face, and the red flicker of radar contacts shines on the radar operator's face. Below, Control is brighter, busier, but eerie in total red except for a few dim green lights on the diving-indicator panel. Red lighting protects the night vision of the bridge watch standers. Lookouts, relieved every twenty minutes to ensure alertness, wear red goggles as they proceed to the crew's Mess for steaming cups of coffee, "blond and sweet" or "black and bitter." Oncoming watch standers—and the captain in the Wardroom—wear the same kind of goggles as they play a hand with special cards that have the suits of hearts and diamonds outlined in black. Red colors cannot be seen under red lighting or through red goggles.

The chief of the watch, "Big John," regales Control Room watch standers with a wild story about his prewar life in the Philippines. Some have heard this yarn before. His full face is animated as he tells of duty in the old P-boats, a 1930s class called after fish whose names start with the letter P. He tells of his running mate Guts, the base at Olongapo, and the native delicacy "beloots" (old egg with embryo). The finale will bring an outburst of laughter that, no doubt, will generate a request from the captain to turn down the volume should "the old man" have turned in.

"Old man" is a strange sobriquet for a submarine skipper barely past thirty. However, only one man on board is older, the chief of the boat, or COB, whose seventeen years of service put him at an ancient thirty-five. He is known as "Old Folks" to the other chiefs in "rest camp" between patrols, but on board the officers and men alike call him "Gunner" in recognition of his gunner's mate rating. The COB is the senior enlisted man on board, and the captain and exec often seek the COB's advice. It is offered freely, with a candor and patience sometimes strained by the inexperience of that new junior officer. The COB is the barometer that gauges the state of the crew, in good situations or bad. He is the interpreter of command policy for his enlisted charges and ombudsman in matters not quite to the general liking. And although each chief works closely with the officer who is his department head, the COB is the main conduit between the Wardroom or "forward battery"—as the sailors refer to the officers—and the crew or "after battery."

The COB passes through Control and interrupts Big John's story briefly. Together, they check the "Christmas tree," or diving panel, whose array of lights shows the status of hull openings, red for shut and green for open. Clean-shaven, wearing clean dungarees, and redolent of "foo foo" (aftershave lotion), he fends off the jeers of the watch standers accusing him of wasting fresh water, pointing out that his shower came from a small tank that collects the condensate from the air-conditioning system. The auxiliaryman on watch, a protector of the freshwater supply, notes the COB's words

▶

"Loading Tin Fish," by Georges Schreiber, depicts a group of enlisted men ready to guide a torpedo in through a loading hatch in the deck of the submarine *Mackerel.* The scene is from 1943 at New London, where *Mackerel* served as a school boat. At 1,200-tons submerged displacement, she was only about half the size of a fleet boat. She was the brainchild of Rear Admiral Thomas Hart, chairman of the Navy's General Board in the late 1930s. He was clearly from the old school and believed small submarines were more desirable than big ones full of newfangled gadgets and luxuries. He won a short-lived victory, but *Mackerel* proved impractical, not up to the demands of the far-reaching, commerce-raiding war in the huge Pacific. And thus it was that she spent the war mostly in New London, teaching hundreds of submariners the skills they would need when they reached a theater of operations where she herself could not go. *(Navy Combat Art Collection, KN-18508)*

with approval but adds, "That recycled sweat might work for you, chief. Just a little too much 'body' in it for me. I'll wait till the freshwater tanks are full." Big John's story resumes as the COB disappears through a watertight door and into the five-man Chief's Quarters for the night.

Minutes later the story hits its climax amid a roar of laughter. Yes, the captain hears the outburst, but rather than sending a message, he arrives on the scene, still fully clothed in rumpled khakis with no rank insignia. Collar devices would have been redundant.

"Hey, you guys, pipe down," says the chief.

With a laugh and a half wave the skipper puts the watch at ease. "John, I'm gonna take a walk through the boat before I try to sleep, okay? Tell the O.D. I'll be up there soon for a gulp of air." Then adjusting his goggles as he enters the white-lighted crew's Mess Hall, he starts a leisurely stroll through each of the compartments of the football-field-length sub. He avoids the open hatch to the battery well in the crew's berthing space—a good place to bark a shin or worse. He shows his past experience as an engineering officer as he makes his way through the engine rooms, feeling a bearing on a motor to make sure that it's not running too hot and looking into the bilges to check their water level. The roar of the diesels and rush of air supplying them causes him to cup a hand about an ear to hear the shouted words of a motor mac whose mouth is only inches away. His chief almost reveres this sweating sailor for his ability to coax results from the new and temperamental water-distilling units. "Shower time tomorrow, Captain. Full

tanks. Not like the old *Tarpon,* right?" A nod of agreement is all that's needed.

As the captain works his way forward, he finds it hard to believe that he is a full commander already. He thought, when he graduated from the Academy, that it would take almost twenty years to get the "scrambled eggs" of that rank on his cap visor. Two years on board the old "Weevie," the battleship *West Virginia,* then sub school. He was a junior officer on a "P-boat," and then came the war. He served a tour as exec on a hot boat with one of the truly heroic skippers. Finally, he has become a hot skipper in his own right, like so many of his Naval Academy class of 1935, a vintage year for Navy Cross submarine drivers. Now, in *Mako,* he's the "old man," or, with admiring affection, "Captain Jack"—but neither within his earshot.

Passing through the Mess Hall, he interrupts the cook, who is pounding out the dough for tomorrow's bread. The captain accepts a roll fresh from the oven with the compliment, "This is great. But you know, nothing tastes as good when you look at it through red glasses."

A few more steps brings him to the radio shack. An officer who has the "coding watch" is busy decoding dozens of messages, and the captain shakes his head in wonder at the volume; *Mako's* task really is not that complex. The normally chatty radioman, who is copying code steadily, grins when the captain teases, "What happened to your Red Sox, Snake? They need Teddy back from his fighter plane, don't they?"

Back in Control he leaves his goggles on the chart desk before climbing the ladder to the Conning Tower. He sees that the radar's operating well, then greets the helmsman.

As he climbs the ladder to the Bridge, the skipper requests, "Permission to come on the Bridge, sir." Even though the boat is his, he is proud to observe this formality, by which the OOD can keep track of just who and how many are on the Bridge. If someone were to come topside and be uncounted, he might be left there when the boat dived. The officer of the deck, of course, replies, "Granted, Captain."

The skipper has a few words with the OOD to amplify the instructions he had written earlier in his Night Order Book. Then he strolls around the periscope shears, or supports, to the "cigarette deck," unused at night because the glow of a burning cigarette could spell detection. He pats the 40-millimeter gun, breathes deeply of the sweet fresh air, and with the words, "Laying below, Bill," starts down to his stateroom for what he hopes will be a few hours of sleep before dawn.

The captain has full confidence in Bill, who is a seasoned submariner, a veteran of five patrols. Bill is *Mako's* engineering officer, and he has the best overall knowledge of the boat's engineering systems and procedures. He also is the best OOD on board. When he has the deck, the 7MC communications speakers—which tie together the Bridge, Conn, Control, Maneuvering, and the Forward and After Torpedo Rooms—has none of the blare and urgency of the new officer's watch. The tone of the new man's messages always conveys a sense of emergency to the crewmen in their bunks—even though the situation is far from tight. But Bill's watch section, number one, is characteristically calm, and that has earned the respect of the entire crew. His quartermaster has twice Bill's patrol experience, and the captain and their shipmates can sleep comfortably, secure in the knowledge that the men standing the four-hour midwatch have the situation in hand, whatever may come up.

The watch sections have a healthy rivalry. Section three will remain at the bottom in its shipmates' esteem until its OOD loses his grip on the panic button. He is known as "George," the standard nickname for the most junior officer, and may be assigned any onerous or trifling task—fitting the saying, "Let George do it." A recent Sub School graduate, he has yet to gain the self-control that comes from knowledge and experience. He is improving slowly, as the skipper and exec work with him patiently, but he's still an easy target for the crew's cartoonist and the butt of a number of practical jokes.

Several days ago George blistered a torpedoman who was, for a break in the routine, standing lookout and planesman watches. The man had moved the stern planes to dive when they should have gone to rise, momentarily taking the boat below periscope depth. Of course, a more-experienced officer would have noted and corrected the mistake before the depth excursion could have occurred.

The crew's retribution was rapid. For the remainder of his diving watch, George suffered from a mysterious inability to control the depth ordered by the OOD. Despite very smooth seas, the damned boat just didn't want to settle down. The planesmen seemed to be doing everything correctly, but George was alternately pumping and flooding, and getting ever more exasperated at his inability to gain control. What his preoccupation kept him from noticing was that ten grinning sailors were moving back and forth between the Forward and After Torpedo Rooms, slowly tilting the boat like a seesaw.

That same evening when George visited the officers' head, or toilet, in the Forward Torpedo Room, he failed to notice that there was a slight pressure left over from the last time the sanitary holding tank had been blown to sea. Coincidentally, the torpedoman on watch "just happened" to be checking the forward bilges then. When George raised the flapper valve, there was a disconcerting "poof" and an instant splattering of one junior officer. The result was a malady jokingly called "freckles."

An hour or so after George had cleaned up every square inch of the small head—and showered—the exec went in to use the facility. With a slight grin he addressed the torpedoman, "Red, is this thing okay?"

The response from the impish, red-haired sailor: "Oh, yes, sir. We tell our friends."

As the skipper moves through Control, heading toward his stateroom, a young auxiliary electrician steps aside and speaks a courteous, "Evening, Captain." He wears the traditional submarine uniform, cotton dungarees, as does the entire crew, including the chiefs. Those senior petty officers proudly disdain the cotton khakis, wearing only a khaki cap in port to denote their paygrade. "Dungaree chiefs" they call themselves, proud of the symbol of their working status.

This electrician's dungarees are a tattered web, testimony to the unusual wear and tear of submarine duty. It is for just this reason that sub pay for years has been called "dungaree money." The captain notes the clothing with a smile and a nod. The electrician has been "hopping gravities," crawling about in the close confines of the main-storage-battery wells and taking the specific gravity of the electrolyte in pilot cells to ascertain the state of charge. He could scarcely avoid dribbles of the sulfuric acid, which has made "holy" dungarees a trademark of electricians since the first submarine.

"Charge about over?"

"Yes sir, Captain. Maneuvering is just about to tell the Bridge and ask permission to go to a float." A "float" would put a generator on the battery bus to keep the battery fully charged as energy was drawn off, just as an automobile generator recharges the battery while a car is running.

"Good. And by the way, you might need a little more protection on those arms. Don't want acid to eat up that new tattoo!"

Big John notes the skipper's comment, and tomorrow the chief electrician will consign the tattered dungarees to new duty as engine-room wiping rags.

The captain picks up his goggles and disappears through the watertight door to the confines of his tiny stateroom, where only a curtain provides a degree of privacy.

With the battery charge completed, the OOD orders the small auxiliary "dinky" engine on the line, and it begins to purr softly, keeping the battery on a fully charged "float" as *Mako* oozes along on the surface at 5 knots. Ballast tanks have been partially flooded, in preparation for a "crash" dive in the event of a surprise attack. The larger swells swish over the teak deck, and *Mako* resembles a broaching or wallowing whale, rather than the shark she becomes when prey draws near.

A report from the Conning Tower destroys the calm of the watch: "Radar contact! Two or three pips bearing two-seven-eight. Range to closest, four-two-oh-double-oh." That means forty-two thousand yards, or twenty-one nautical miles.

Bill turns the sub to point toward the contact, hoping to get a better radar return while minimizing *Mako*'s own profile.

The captain, who was still awake in his stateroom, is at the radar in seconds. Another good bearing shows slight movement to the left. "Looks good, Bill. Couple of contacts coming out of the islands, moving southwest, I think. Get your radar tracking party on and start an end around that way yourself. I'll be at the radar a few minutes."

The 1MC speaker system reaches all compartments: "Station the radar tracking party." Out come the most skilled radar operator and off-watch quartermasters. George mans plot because this is a skill in which he has shown real proficiency.

Bill orders, "Control, put the low-pressure blower on all main ballast tanks. Blow safety and negative dry." Following doctrine, the OOD is lightening *Mako*, making her float as high as possible to get maximum speed. This will enable her to pull ahead of the targets. With a surge of power, her four diesel engines drive her at more than 20 knots through the glassy sea. This is much faster than she can go in the daytime, when submerged operations on battery power slow her to a maximum speed of less than 8 knots. The night also gives her the same concealment that submergence does.

Like her namesake, *Mako* begins hunting her prey.

On the Bridge, Bill feels a twinge of apprehension as he observes the submarine's long white wake. Even in the complete blackness it seems to him that any enemy within several thousand yards could readily see the slash of foam. The lookouts and quartermaster are now silent and tense, straining to detect any sign of the enemy: a telltale wake, a flash of white, or a cigarette's glow.

Bill's leading chief asks permission to come up, then tells him that the Fairbanks-Morse diesel engines are running fine. "If we need it, we can pick her up to 138 percent, sir. The railroads run 'em at 2,200 horsepower, not 1,600 like us!" But having noted some sparks coming from the number three engine when they got to that power while dodging escorts during the last patrol, Bill had backed off then, and he won't succumb this time.

"Battle Stations, Torpedo!" calls *Mako*'s crew to action. Within seconds the men are at their stations.

"I have the conn," the captain announces.

Bill reports to the helmsman, "The captain has the conn." The helmsman repeats that to verify that he understands.

The captain intends to bore in on the target's flank to ensure maximum damage along its entire length. The TDC operator periodically calls out torpedo track and torpedo run—the distance in yards the first torpedo will run before hitting the target.

"Left full rudder." The captain orders a turn in toward the targets, and the sub snaps into a steady heel as the helmsman puts the rudder over. Pointing directly at an escort to reduce his silhouette, he lowers his speed just a bit, hoping to diminish the white wake. In the still night, the diesels still roar thunderously. The Bridge watch standers are certain that the Japanese can hear them, but the escort slides by. Now for that fat target.

The order, "Open outer doors forward" places the torpedo battery in full readiness.

"Range 1,800 yards," radar reports. Maybe too close.

A lookout screams, "Torpedo wake bearing zero-two-zero!" A white phosphorescent wake is ribboning almost directly at *Mako*.

The captain's urgent command, "Right full rudder! All ahead flank!" turns the bow to present the sharpest aspect to this new and most deadly threat, and the extra speed increases the sub's agility. More torpedoes may be on the way.

The torpedo's whine is heard distinctly throughout the boat as it roars down the port side. Not one of *Mako*'s crew has heard this sound so close before. Yet the "old man" turns the sub gently left, boring in, focused on the kill, cool even while death is screaming down *Mako*'s side.

"Final bearing and shoot!"—the captain transmits a bearing of the large ship's midsection to the TDC. "Bearing, mark!" inserts the firing bearing and precipitates a series of shudders from a salvo of four of *Mako*'s finest steam torpedoes.

The starboard lookout reports another torpedo wake well clear off the starboard beam.

The fire-control party feverishly prepares to shoot the remaining two fish forward and four aft.

"Right full rudder," orders the captain. This will take *Mako* a bit close to an escort but get her away from the one she slid by.

Suddenly, a terrific explosion erupts to starboard, and flames leap high in the darkness. "What the hell?" forms in many minds at once. Things had been going too fast to question the torpedo's source, but now the escort is blown to bits—and not by one of *Mako*'s torpedoes.

As she swings clear to starboard, a series of detonations shakes the night and rips open the vitals of *Mako*'s target. Home run!

Racing for what he hopes will be concealment in a dense rainsquall ten miles to the east, the skipper tries to sort out what has happened. Most likely, *Mako*'s buddy sub in the adjacent area had the same idea and the same target, but missed the merchant and got the escort—and almost got *Mako*!

Tearing along at "railroad power" now, tired and drained, the "old man" feels the part implied by his nickname. He relates his theory to the exec, who has joined him on the Bridge.

With a wry smile, the exec whistles softly and says, "Captain—like the men say—we don't want you if you're not lucky! Cup of coffee?"

"KOG"—The Kindly Old Gentleman

A spacious and lovely apartment in Arlington, Virginia, looks out upon a vista that includes a new shopping mall. To the right in a jungle of concrete called Crystal City lie many-storied office buildings, many occupied by industries that want to be near at hand when the military decides on the specifications for their weapons systems. Farther to the right lie offices in which the Department of Defense evaluates the work of defense contractors. To the left lies the heart of the military establishment, the "five-sided puzzle factory," the Pentagon, from which the requirements for all military systems must emanate. In this apartment lived a man who had tremendous influence over many of the organizations that the apartment overlooks.

The man was Admiral Hyman G. Rickover, known by a variety of nicknames or epithets to the corporations, the officers, the designers, and the engineers with whom he worked. From the early days of development of USS *Nautilus,* the first nuclear submarine, he became known as the "KOG," for "kindly old gentleman." It was a rather incongruous and jestful term, indeed, for he evoked awe, fear, and apprehension in those people who fell within his sphere of influence.

In the apartment today his widow, Eleanore Rickover, lives amid a plethora of memorabilia attesting to his more than sixty years as a naval officer, as an engineer, and ultimately as the developer of fleets of nuclear-powered ships. All of them bear the stamp of his approval, and because of the rigid specifications under which they were constructed, tested, and operated, it was a very personal stamp. On the walls hang photographs of the admiral with his boats and men. In a hallway photographs show him with the various U.S. presidents under whom he served. In one unused room are cartons, yet unpacked, full of mementos that deserve the cataloging of a skilled museum curator.

In one corner Mrs. Rickover points out a polished hardwood chair that has acquired the patina of legend because of its shortened front legs. The admiral used this chair in his earliest interviews of the candidates who were being considered for nuclear propulsion training. Rickover employed a system of stress interviews for every officer or civilian engineer who wished to enter his program, a practice that he continued throughout his days as the lord of nuclear propulsion. Sitting on the chair, one found oneself sliding forward, an experience that was truly disconcerting in itself, but even more so while one was trying to respond sensibly to a barrage of questions.

Many of these were designed to cause soul-searching, anger, or embarrassment, often belittling perceived accomplishments or pointing up character weaknesses. Few who were interviewed were not off balance.

His reputation led one to expect a large, imposing figure, bombastic perhaps. Not so. The body of the man was small, bony, even frail. But there was nothing at all small about his spirit, which was imposing and indomitable. His focus was total. Every waking hour—and perhaps even his dreams—centered upon the task at hand, that of producing the most nearly perfect ships and propulsion plants that could be built. The first nuclear-powered sub, *Nautilus,* completed in a brief four years under his supervision, is a tribute to the fierce determination and organizational genius of one small giant of an engineer.

The totality of his control was part of the reason for his success. He somehow kept track of where each of the people he relied upon was during every waking moment. "Get me So-and-so!" he would shout in a high, nasal voice that was immediately recognizable to submarine captains and other subordinates wherever nuclear work was in progress. Somehow, his tireless secretaries would find "So-and-so" in minutes. For example, one of his leading people was driving on vacation from Washington to Florida. Somewhere in one of the Caroli-

nas a highway patrolman waved him to a stop. No ticket—just a smile and a message, "You are to call Admiral Rickover."

On another occasion the commanding officer of the nuclear-training unit in Idaho heard himself paged as he passed through the Salt Lake City airport. When he got to the telephone, he heard the admiral ask with no salutation, "You have had a steam-generator problem at the A1W plant! Doesn't it chagrin you to know that when you are in Washington, visiting me, that your people let you down?"

A bit of abrasive conversation followed. Then the officer, who looked forward to returning to command at sea, added, "Admiral, the best thing for you to do is to fire me! Why don't you do that?"

The reply, with a disguised chuckle, was, "Hell no! That's what you want. For every mistake you or your guys make, I'm giving you three more months at Idaho!"

There *was* a sense of humor in the man, but only those who were to gain some degree of rapport with him were ever to sort it out from his energy and drive. As one who became as close as any was to say, "Yes, he can be pleasant, and he has a sense of humor, but you have to keep a distance. It's something like petting a panther!"

It is difficult for one not in the nuclear-propulsion program to fully grasp the totality of his control. His system of personally interviewing and selecting candidates grew from his knowledge that the Navy's personnel evaluations are tainted by favoritism or the inability of a senior to report objectively on one with whom he lives and works daily. In too many cases for the good of the system, an officer may play golf or squash with that senior or even marry a relative.

The admiral also devised a system of accountability that was without parallel. While an immediate telephone report, directly to him, was mandatory in the case of any problem or incident, subordinates were required to write weekly progress

◀

President Harry S. Truman begins a new era in submarine propulsion when he inscribes his initials on the keel of *Nautilus,* the world's first nuclear-powered submarine. The ceremony took place at the Electric Boat shipyard at Groton, Connecticut, in June 1952. Flanking the president are John Jay Hopkins of General Dynamics and Secretary of the Navy Dan Kimball. The name *Nautilus* came from an earlier U.S. submarine, from a sea creature, and also from the name of an imaginary undersea craft in Jules Verne's classic 1870 work of science fiction, *20,000 Leagues Under the Sea*. A league is a measure of distance equal to two or three miles. The deepest point of the earth's oceans is seven miles deep, thus two and a fraction leagues. Twenty thousand leagues would put the old *Nautilus* a quarter of the way to the moon. With a bit of whimsy, we might observe that Captain Nemo was not only the world's first submariner but its first astronaut as well. *(Electric Boat Company, courtesy Submarine Force Library and Museum)*

▲

(Left) As a tribute to Admiral Rickover, the "father of the nuclear Navy," the engineering hall at the U.S. Naval Academy is named Rickover Hall. Inside stands a bust sculpted by Paul Wegner, son of a longtime deputy of Rickover. Midshipmen rub the prominent nose for good luck, causing it to shine.

▲

The first reactor-plant prototype was constructed in the desert near Arco, Idaho. It proved the design of *Nautilus*'s plant and has provided training for submarine crews for decades.

letters to him, outlining trends and lesser problems. The requirement extended to the captains of boats under construction or undergoing overhaul, the managers of the industries doing nuclear work, and even lesser training managers and engineer officers of prototype plants. Letters from skippers were "encouraged" after long patrols so that they could inform him about the performance of the propulsion plant. Naturally, this system generated great interest from any supervisor, who would wonder what a subordinate was reporting that he had glossed over.

Rickover's ironclad methodology has spread throughout the Navy as major surface ships and all submarines have become nuclear powered. The selection and training of personnel receive high priority, perhaps the highest priority of the entire program. This emphasis has resulted not necessarily in trouble-free, but certainly accident-free construction and operation of scores of complex reactor plants. Strict maintenance procedures, frequent rehearsals, rigid checks and balances, formality, and, finally, the closest supervision and adherence to approved procedures contribute to the great success and confidence the officers and men display in the technological marvels they take to sea.

One recalls the words of Mrs. Rickover: when asked for her recollections as to just what the admiral seemed to admire most, she said, "As you know, he rode each ship on its first sea trials; he felt responsible. When we talked after such trips, he often would tell me that the thing which impressed him most was the superb, *absolutely superb* performance of the very young sailors and officers, many at sea for the first time in their lives."

Today a prominent academic building, Rickover Hall, stands at the U.S. Naval Academy. In this building midshipmen receive education in an engineering curriculum that the admiral helped form when years earlier he had criticized the conduct of education at the academy. In the entranceway stands a simple and beautifully finished bronze bust, sculpted by Paul Wegner, the son of one of Rickover's most trusted and valued subordinates and longtime deputy. The sculpture is a mute but lasting tribute to this "father of the nuclear Navy." It seems most fitting that the bust looks out upon the youth of the Navy.

A veteran of the nuclear Navy, one who might be termed a pioneer, visits Rickover Hall and is amused watching one after another midshipman pause to rub the prominent nose of the bust, a practice that has given that feature a rich shine. The veteran nuke makes a silent wish that something of the "KOG" rubs off onto those doing the rubbing.

▲

The attack subs *Hyman G. Rickover* (SSN-709) and *Baton Rouge* (SSN-689) during a Christmas maintenance and leave period in Norfolk, Virginia. Named in honor of the eminent admiral who is accorded the title "father of the nuclear Navy," *Rickover* represents a departure from the practice of naming *Los Angeles*–class subs for cities.

◀

For centuries, men searched for the fabled Northwest Passage through the Arctic. As depicted by artist Walter Bollendonk, the nuclear-powered attack submarine *Seadragon* finally found it. In the summer of 1960 *Seadragon* left Portsmouth, New Hampshire, for Pearl Harbor, her new home port. In the process she made the first submerged transit of the Northwest Passage, going via Parry Channel and Lancaster Sound. Her skipper, Commander George P. Steele, used Edward Parry's 1819 journal as a guide. The submarine continued her journey by traveling through the Beaufort Sea to the geographic North Pole, then headed for Alaska and finally Hawaii. In 1962 *Seadragon* made a second cruise to the Arctic, this time rendezvousing with the submarine *Skate*, which had departed from New London, Connecticut. The two subs met under the ice and continued to the North Pole. *(Navy Combat Art Collection)*

The Stealth of Silence

NUCLEAR ATTACK SUBMARINES

I n 1950 Captain Hyman G. Rickover explained the idea of a nuclear-powered submarine to officers at Groton, Connecticut. When asked when the idea could become a reality, he replied, "Four years, if I'm in charge." He was in charge—and *Nautilus* went to sea on 17 January 1955. It was a revolution in submarine design, and Rickover, *Nautilus,* and her handpicked skipper and crew did a magnificent job in selling virtually the entire Congress on the value of nuclear propulsion. So busy was *Nautilus* in the fast and furious pace of carting dignitaries to sea that the hard-working crew griped that the USS before the name stood for "Underway Saturday and Sunday."

Seawolf, the second nuclear sub, paved the way for the development of new tactics to use her speed. *Skate* and *Skipjack* classes followed in short order, the latter showing the whale-shaped hull and single propeller that all future U.S. subs would use. Magnificent submarines all, they afforded unprecedented habitability compared with their diesel-powered predecessors. One old-time chief petty officer, riding *Seawolf* for a day of high-speed operations and torpedo shooting, declared in awe when he left the boat, "Sir, she's a goddamn Cadillac submarine" and volunteered for nuclear duty the next day. One of *Seawolf's* first junior officers changed to fresh, pressed khakis for dinner in the wardroom one night during sea trials, explaining, "You know, on *Blenny* we were always kinda dirty and oily, but this is like being in a fine hotel—you feel that you should dress for dinner."

These revolutionary boats offered living spaces of comparative luxury, air revitalization that provided independence from the earth's atmosphere, and the ability to produce a virtually unlimited supply of fresh water. The nuclear power plant could run for years without refueling. Nevertheless, it was the tactical capabilities of these submarines that were the most important advancement. From the start, it was obvious that *Nautilus*

◀

Sunset in Norfolk, Virginia, silhouettes the destroyer force and submarines of Squadron Six, with USS *Hammerhead* (SSN-663) in the foreground.

alone, with her improved sensors, speed, and endurance, could have destroyed the entire Japanese fleet. Yet recent submarines, with their advanced sensors, state of quieting, and efficiency of propulsion, make *Nautilus* and her earlier cohorts look like plow horses.

Despite any improvements, the basic role of the attack submarine has remained the same as that of the World War I diesel boats—sinking ships. And in pursuit of that goal, even the stealthiest nuclear-powered boats have adopted ever-more-capable weapons, including missiles. Along with new weapons, of course, have come new ideas about how to use them, and recent submarine crews have followed in the wake of the *Seawolf's* men, developing new tactics that, for example, permit submarines to work closely with surface forces or, as seen in the Gulf war, to project power over land with long-range missiles. The modern attack submarine can truly identify with the motto, "Any place, any time."

The liberty sections of USS *Brooklyn's* crew have returned to the ship, most carrying bags of clothes, some favorite snacks, toilet articles for a month or two, and other personal items. The newly commissioned attack sub, one of the improved *Los Angeles,* or 688-I, class, is about to go to sea. As she lies at her moorings on the Elizabeth River in Norfolk, the bulk of her bow is impressive. She projects a different appearance from the boats of the original *Los Angeles* class. A rubberlike coating of anechoic tiles, freshly painted black, covers most of the hull and will serve to deaden the pings of opposing active sonar and thus reduce *Brooklyn's* detectability.

Brooklyn also lacks the distinctive "wings" on the sail, the fairwater planes that control her depth when submerged. Her planes are on the bow, the location previously favored prior to the adoption of the *Albacore*-type hull, which was the perfectly round, whale-shaped sub design. The 688s were originally not intended to surface through ice, but this will be possible in the last twenty-three 688s because of the installation of bow planes that can be rigged in or out.

Also installed in the bow is a deadly battery of twelve vertical launch tubes, for the Tomahawk long-range cruise missiles.

The order, "Station the Maneuvering Watch" is passed on the general announcing system. Passageways come alive with activity as sailors move to their sea-detail stations to get the sub underway. The passageways are congested because space is not wasted simply to facilitate walking about. A submariner subconsciously turns sideways or pulls up to wait until a shipmate passes. (Diesel submariners recall an amusing moment in a TV special years ago when Esther Williams, a curvaceous movie actress, called attention to her difficulty—especially turned sideways—in passing delighted sailors in passageways much narrower than today's.)

Men who will have stations topside, line handlers and phone talkers, put on orange life jackets. Another dons a diver's wet suit; he's the swimmer, ready if necessary to leap into the river and rescue a line handler who might fall overboard.

The announcement, "Testing Alarms" on the 1MC speaker triggers a cacophony of noises: sirens, beeps, and gongs. Old-time submariners are surprised and a bit chagrined that the "Ah-oooo-gah" of the diving alarm they knew has degenerated to a flat musical tone that carries none of the spark and excitement of the old Klaxon.

Brooklyn's reactor has been critical for several hours, and the turbines have been jacked over and then rolled with steam. The freshwater tanks were topped off earlier, and a final load of fresh milk is carried aboard as cranes lift the brow, or gangway. Line handlers pull in the lines, and a long blast on the whistle and the shifting of the flag signal that the sub is under way. Tugs sound short toots, assisting the OOD in backing the sub clear of her mooring. Soon she enters the Elizabeth River and settles on a course heading out of the channel. The tugs cast off, and she picks up speed.

Shortly after *Brooklyn* is clear of the pier, the word is passed, "Rig ship for dive," and the crew begins a lengthy, meticulous process. Each compartment has a checkoff sheet, or "bill," that lists in excruciating detail the valves, lineups, and conditions that must be checked open, shut, in power or manual position, free to operate, clear of interference, full, empty, so much pressure, etc. The watch stander in the compartment checks off each item on the bill, and then an officer also runs through the list. Only then is the compartment reported to Control as "rigged for dive." The ship will not be submerged until every compartment is fully rigged and checked. Subs have been sunk and people have died as a result of one or another failure to rig for dive properly. Submariners will cite, for example, the sinking of the U.S. sub *Squalus* off New Hampshire in 1939 because of rags that were fouling the large main induction valve.

In the same containers with the rig-for-dive bill are many other detailed bills for a number of evolutions or emergency situations: fire, collision, flooding, toxic gas, and others. Crew members consult each one during *Brooklyn*'s frequent drills. However, the state of training is such that watch standers and the men who happen to be in the affected compartment at the time perform the major actions on the list within seconds. Then they consult the bill for completeness. During the drills, the "large holes" seem to receive the earliest and fastest attention. The watertight doors and ventilation-line flapper valves between compartments seal off most water, air, smoke, or gas.

Now, having passed beyond the Virginia Capes, *Brooklyn* enters the Atlantic Ocean. The navigator has finished piloting the narrow channel, and the Maneuvering Watch is secured. As the normal steaming watch is set, the crew can feel the sub roll slightly. One can get seasick in a sub, even in the large missile boats, at least when surfaced. Ocean swells can produce a fairly good roll at periscope depth, although compared with the crashing and slamming of World War II diesel boats in rough seas, these modern subs are indeed user-friendly. Submariners have reported rolls of 30 degrees even at 300-foot depth in severe storms, hurricanes, and typhoons. Normally, though, the ride is smooth once the boat has submerged.

At this point the radar operator is actively tracking a ship ahead, a destroyer entering port on an opposite course from *Brooklyn*'s. Using a plot in the complex fire-control system, the operator reports the closest point of approach, or CPA, to the officer of the deck. If there is not enough passing room to suit his standard for safety, the OOD may alter course or speed or both to give the destroyer a wider berth. The captain receives a report on the destroyer's position; at sea his life becomes a relentless flow of reports—all course and speed changes, ship contacts and their CPAs if they pose potential problems, and

This view shows a colorful ceremony at Newport News Shipbuilding Company, in which USS *Albany* slides down the building ways after being launched by Mrs. Henry Kissinger. While the laying of the keel marks the actual "birth" of a ship, the launching is the first momentous occasion in her life. The launching ceremony is a tradition that reaches back four thousand years, and the practice of using wine or champagne as a toast had its inception in the pagan mind but was dignified by the early Christian church. For the last century and a half, the tradition throughout the world has been that a woman, known as the sponsor, christens the ship, breaking a bottle of spirits on the bow to send the vessel on her way. For many years this was an honor accorded primarily to the wives of naval officers, but with the advent of nuclear-powered ships and their political implications, and the attendant media attention, the wives of political figures have lately been dominant as sponsors. ▶

hundreds of other items that may affect the operation or readiness of his boat. Submariners exercise great caution on the surface—and for good reason. Low in the water, they are a poor radar target and are difficult to see, particularly at night. Submarines have little positive buoyancy, so the results would be disastrous if they were sliced open by another ship.

As an example of such caution, consider the time in 1962 when *Scorpion* was returning to Norfolk just as an entire squadron of destroyers was converging on the port. It was just before dawn. Although *Scorpion* had the right of way, the line of ships was bearing down on her. She flashed signals on the searchlight and announced herself on the underwater telephone, but to no avail. With shallow water to her right and precious little room astern, *Scorpion* backed and backed while each destroyer in turn passed a scant hundred yards or less across her bow. The destroyer commodore's subsequent investigation revealed neither log entries nor recollections by his watch standers of a submarine sighting. One had noted "a small fishing boat to starboard." The sub captain requested an urgent audience with the vice admiral who commanded Atlantic Fleet submarines and got fast action. The admiral had been contemplating installing a flashing orange anticollision light on his subs to alert other ships that a vulnerable vessel was in their midst. The new light was ordered for all subs within a day.

The Fathometer confirms the navigator's estimate for *Brooklyn's* time of arrival at the 40-fathom curve, where the eastern continental shelf of the United States slopes off into the depths. It's time to dive. The Bridge watch shuts the "clamshell" doors over the Bridge opening. That streamlines the top of the bridge and ensures that the water passing over the opening won't make any noise. The dive itself is not exciting compared with those of earlier decades: there's no need today for the fast dives of the past, when submarines patrolled mainly on the surface and had to be prepared to dive quickly to escape hostile aircraft.

Once *Brooklyn* is down, the diving officer, an experienced chief petty officer, is responsible for properly trimming the boat. He ensures that his planesmen move the bow planes and stern planes to maintain both a neutral "bubble"—the bow-to-stern angle on the sub, measured traditionally by a clinometer, which is a liquid-filled glass-tube arc with an air bubble inside—and the ordered depth. The diving planes place a force on the boat as she moves through the water to make her rise toward the surface or fall toward the bottom. Combining these forces with the weights from the bow, stern, or amidships ballast tanks, the diving officer pumps ballast among the various tanks until the boat requires no plane angle to maintain depth at slow speed. Increased speed produces more force on the planes, giving the diving officer greater control. An angle on the sub makes use of the planing forces of the entire deck or bottom to move up or down more rapidly.

While a few degrees of angle is a comfortable way to change depth, an ordered 30 degrees at high speed makes one suck in one's stomach, particularly if a large amount of rudder is used to turn the ship to another course at the same time. A submarine is different from an aircraft because a maneuvering boat produces G forces too small to hold one in a seat; one hears the sound of crashing dishes and unstowed articles, and one needs to hang on! In fact, in the first subs to engage in high-speed maneuvers, crewmen soon discovered that subway-type hand straps were a necessity, and today's subs are also equipped with seat belts for the planesmen.

▲

The sub tender *Emory S. Land* with some of the *Los Angeles*–class subs of Squadron Eight at Christmas. The diesel-engine exhaust of *Jacksonville* forms fog in the cold evening.

The crew of USS *Pasadena* has difficulty staying in neat lines on deck as the boat accelerates to 30 knots while sliding down the building ways of Electric Boat Company in Groton, Connecticut, into the Thames River. The boat's bow has just received the traditional champagne christening by sponsor Pauline Trost, wife of then Chief of Naval Operations Admiral Carlisle Trost, a renowned submariner.

▶

▲
A familiar landmark at
Submarine Base Pearl
Harbor is the 110-foot
training tank. For years
submariners were required
to requalify annually in
escape from the bottom of
the column of water, using
first the Momsen lung,
later Steinke hoods and
free-ascent devices. Such
training has been discon-
tinued in the U.S. Navy.

▲
A Christmas sunset transforms Submarine Squadron Eight
and the tender *Emory S. Land* into a golden fleet at piers on the
Elizabeth River, Norfolk.

An Elizabeth River pilot joins the captain on the Bridge of *Jefferson City* as she makes her way back to Norfolk, Virginia. ▶

Submarine tenders perform countless repair and maintenance jobs to assure the proper operation of the submarine force. Tender crews include welders, wood and metal workers, molders, doctors, dentists—everything a crew of a submarine or its machinery may need.

▲

The tough and hot job of pouring molten metal into molds to make cast-iron or bronze parts is a "man's job," except that here in USS *Emory Land,* a tender that maintains subs, one of those holding a substantial amount of the weight is a woman.

▲
The State Pier and water tower in the heart of New London, Connecticut, has been a landmark for generations of submariners who have operated from the pier. Some tenders have been moored there for so long that sailors jokingly remark that the ships could not depart because they lie fixed on a shoal of their own coffee grounds. USS *Fulton,* with the *Los Angeles*–class *Philadelphia* moored alongside, has been older than the senior captains who have commanded her for many years. The *Groton,* another 688-class sub, is moored to the pier.

Torpedomen at the Mark 48 torpedo shop in San Diego maintain and check the supply of torpedoes. For years a man's job, the rating now includes a number of women.　　　▶

In electrical shop of tender USS *Fulton* a petty officer completes a task of rewiring a submarine motor.
▼

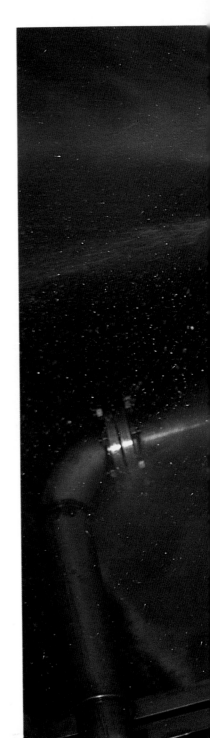

Now the operations begin. Perhaps they will be only local exercises, with *Brooklyn* serving as opposition for the training of U.S. antisubmarine forces. Perhaps there will be operations in direct support of an aircraft-carrier battle group, in which the boat will provide warning and protection against enemy shadowing units or, in a hostile situation, against attackers. Often the mission will require a long transit, perhaps at high speed to show a presence or exert force in a hot spot. Alternatively, the transit speed may be moderate, with the boat remaining absolutely undetected, perhaps for an intelligence-gathering mission.

Depending upon the situation, the submarine may or may not slow down at specified intervals during the transit to raise antennas to receive radio messages. With today's satellite-communications capabilities, such slowing requires only a few minutes, compared with the tens of minutes to hours necessary in the old days, when hand-keyed Morse-code transmission and reception were the norm. Even radio signals relayed by non-satellite means now come at high speed, and digital processors rather than men handle the radio traffic. When operational commanders want a sub to get some place in minimum time, they will make special communications arrangements to extend the time between mandatory radio-reception periods.

The captain announces that the job for today's operation is one of surveillance, of listening for specific activities and shipping of interest to the United States. The job could be monitoring or photographing evidence of contraband shipments to some country, collecting intelligence on a particular ship's characteristics or noises, or perhaps assisting in intercepting drug traffic. Where? It matters little to the crew, other than that in some places it would be far easier to detect the boat, and thus the crew would need to take greater care in avoiding noise and to be more alert in detecting quiet contacts. But the modus operandi is *always* to remain undetected, and to pick up the other sub or surface ship before she detects *Brooklyn*.

Because the emphasis is on quietness, officers and chiefs inspect the compartments for the proper stowage of spares, supplies, and equipment. A can of coffee that touches a unit of rotating machinery, for example, can conduct the noise to the hull and beyond—a sonic "short circuit." A compartment was painted in the last upkeep period, and the rubber sound isolation on the equipment foundations was covered with masking tape to prevent paint from deteriorating the rubber. Has the tape been removed? If not, another sound short could give the boat away. Monitors are used continuously on board subs to check for unwanted noise, and all watches and supervisors conduct follow-up inspections daily.

Another precaution is taken. To remain undetected, the sub must not use the active pinging sonar, must not transmit on radio or the underwater telephone, and must not use the radars. The men can be trusted, but they can make mistakes

and inadvertently energize some "noisy" equipment, so supervisors pull out and stow the fuses to this gear. To what lengths will these men go to avoid noise? One new captain of an SSN en route to an intelligence-gathering mission was startled to see a senior lieutenant rummaging through the garbage to be ejected into the ocean. The officer was making absolutely certain that no intact bottles or light bulbs were in the trash because the sea pressure would crush them as they sank, and the noise could be a dead giveaway.

Soon *Brooklyn* settles down to the routine that the crew will follow for weeks. The first day out is a sleepy one, and most skippers have learned that the sea's motion, even if slight, and the new work and watch-standing tempo are good reasons for an easy day with little on the schedule besides settling in.

While the old diesel boats were much like other ships, cruising for the most part on the surface where a good number of the crew could see the ocean and the sky daily, the nukes offer no such scenic tours. *Brooklyn* cruises smoothly, noiselessly even at 20-knot speed, gliding up or down to use the ocean's thermal layers to avoid being detected by opposition sonar. Differences in water temperature create these layers, which

In highly specialized wet trainers at Submarine Training Facility San Diego, flooding casualties are simulated and realistically carried out to stress the capabilities of students and crews of submarines. Water is caused to leak through splits in the piping at 200-psi pressure. ▶

refract, or trap, sound waves and serve as curtains behind which subs can hide.

An attack submarine's maneuverability is much like that of an airplane. Indeed, when a hot SSN moves in for an attack against a carrier or destroyer, she is most like a fighter plane, able to fly "wing on wing" with fast ships. A basic difference exists, though. If something breaks or malfunctions, submariners can't land and change a unit, switch planes, or eject. What you see is what you've got; make it last or fix it—and that's the role of the technically trained crew—or go without for weeks to months.

Another basic is often lost to many observers. Submariners don't send or receive mail while at sea. Nor are there any phone calls in this marvelous age of satellites and computerized wonders. A sailor under the sea can occasionally receive a "family gram," a radio message no more than fifty words long, but he can't reply. World news and sports are received on regular press broadcasts that are printed up for the crew's reading. Generally, there are no port visits. Things at home change during the time a sailor is underwater. A baby cuts teeth, a child learns to walk, an old car dies. A culture may come and go; in the late 1950s when *Seawolf* returned after setting the then

world submergence record of sixty days, the crew stared in fascination at the sight of people everywhere furiously rotating plastic hoops about their gyrating hips—hula hoops!

Some years back a submarine admiral was flying in a small jet as a guest of Commander in Chief Strategic Air Command. Asked if he had ever tried his hand at flying a peppy little jet—and he hadn't—he was invited by the general to fly the plane. So he did. Other Air Force passengers noted that the naval officer seldom looked outside, relying heavily on instruments. The CinC laughed and said, "Hell, fellows. He's a submariner. He's on instruments all the time."

Gyros and accelerometers provide courses to be steered and dead-reckoning inputs for geographical positioning. Sonar detects and tracks ship contacts without the sub's ever sighting them. Sonar also discriminates fish, whales, shrimp, and rainsqualls from ship contacts, and instruments measure water temperatures at the various depths to plot the shadow zones, the optimal depths for hiding or for detecting quiet targets. If desired, active sonar can be used to prosecute an attack. Those who read Tom Clancy's *The Hunt for Red October* will recall the talented sonarman Jonesy, who was a real artist at deciphering the signals provided by his electronic sensors. Jonesy has many real-life counterparts in today's submarine force.

Brooklyn does have periscopes, extraordinarily good ones, but their use is not a steady diet unless and until the boat is on station for a surveillance mission. The officer of the deck, the navigator, and the skipper or exec are usually the only ones to use the periscopes. Very few of the 150-man crew ever get a squint at the outside. As Alaskan dogsled mushers are wont to say, "The scenery changes only for the lead dog."

As the first underway watch section assumes stations, an observer would note another change from the in-port routine. Dungarees and khakis have been shed, and the entire crew now wears a one-piece, synthetic, blue uniform known as a "poopy suit." Originally designed in 1958 to help alleviate a problem that was specific to the new Polaris submarines, these jumpsuits are also now used in SSNs on patrol. The Polaris boats' long-duration dives without changing air produced rivers of condensate in the living space where moist air hit the cold hull. One result was that the clothes inside the lockers located against the hull became dripping wet or moldy. While modifications were made to insulate the hull and to permit the circulation of air-conditioned air into previously stagnant areas,

the solution was to reduce the amount of moisture placed into the subs' atmosphere, and the place to start was with the biggest offenders, the boats' clothes dryers.

Tests proved that synthetic fabrics would retain only 7 percent of the moisture carried to the dryers by cotton dungarees. An innovative staff officer, impressed at the time by a perceived need to man battle stations rapidly in the new missile boats—later proved baloney—specified the design for a new uniform. His idea was that a man could jump out of his bunk and into this suit in one motion. To accommodate other needs, it was provided with a drop seat. Among sailors, it became known as the "poopy suit," later redesigned as a cumbersome jumpsuit without a stern hatch.

Throughout *Brooklyn's* transit to station, the days are filled with training and casualty drills. The captain initially stresses noisy exercises so that he can omit those once on station, when absolute quiet is required. One thing is evident—the training is never over, and the qualification or requalification is never complete. At any hour young sailors and officers can be taken through some system or compartment and cross-examined in detail by petty officers and officers. For key qualifications, the final examiners are the captain and exec. The officers

▶

Under a steady cold rain, a solitary workman sandblasts the hull of USS *Billfish* (SSN-676) in the floating dry dock *Shippingport* at Submarine Base Groton, Connecticut. The actions of the photographer, a retired admiral, strained the credulity of the patrolling sentry, who found it difficult to fathom the sight of an umbrella-protected camera at night.

▶

(Top inset) The floating dry dock *Arco* floods down to permit the departure of USS *Salt Lake City* upon completion of repairs to her underwater hull fittings. The bulbous bow contains the sensitive sonar system. Floating dry docks are mobile vessels that make possible hull work in overseas bases. The walls are actually large tanks that are floodable, permitting the dry dock to "sink" to receive submarines, which rest on wood blocks as the dry dock is pumped out.

▶

(Bottom inset) USS *Houston*, a *Los Angeles*–class attack sub, rests on keel blocks in a floating dry dock in San Diego. The crew has decorated the bow in enthusiasm for the Army-Navy football rivalry as game day draws near. A Navy victory provided testimony of the drawing's effectiveness.

◀

Realistic training in fighting fires makes use of training facilities that are constructed to duplicate the interior of a submarine. Computers control the heat, flame, and smoke and cut off the fuel in case of emergency.

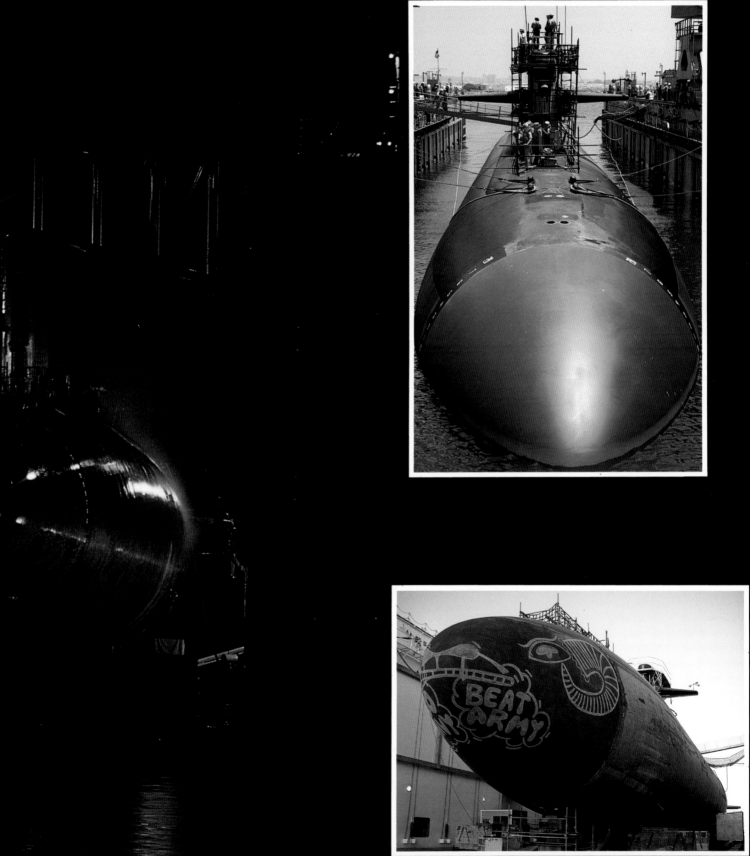

and leading petty officers emphasize realism in the drills. In casualty drills that call for an emergency shutdown of the reactor and steam plant, for example, the reactor really is "scrammed"; the shutdown isn't merely simulated. In certain drills, men even enter the shut-down reactor compartment, as they would if a real casualty occurred and repairs were needed.

Brooklyn's skipper assumed command three months ago, relieving a captain who was known for meticulous adherence to procedures but for taking no risks. Drills had been pre-announced and stressed simulation rather than the actual manipulation of systems. Lethargy had replaced the talented crew's enthusiasm.

The new skipper had whipped up a storm the first time he called away battle stations, shouting and cursing the long delays. Immediately, he had met with each watch section to point out the rules of the new regime and announce the setting of a wartime footing for the boat. He had denounced the softness of "this new generation" and highlighted his remarks with an episode from the Korean War, in which only a small percentage of U.S. Army troops, though faced with death or defeat, fired their rifles at the oncoming hordes of Communist troops. "What was their problem? Simple! Softness—still tied to their momma's apron strings. 'Momism!' Momism! Now, I want to kick the momism the hell off this boat, starting now!" He had repeated the message for each of the three sections, with increasing intensity.

Then battle stations and several other evolutions had been called away and proceeded with amazing smoothness and speed, and as the days passed the crew's performance got only better. A week later the exec came into the captain's stateroom and said, "Hey, Captain. Your 'momism' is catching on. I just heard the leading machinist raising hell with his troops: 'Come on, get moving! Your momism's showing!'"

The sequel, which occurred a week ago, shows the canny irreverence of a submarine crew. Most boats celebrate a crewman's birthday with a beautiful sheet cake, cut and served by the honoree in the Mess Hall, and *Brooklyn's* cooks were especially gifted at decorating a cake with pastoral scenes. But on the skipper's birthday, a horde of delighted sailors greeted him with a cake frosted as simply as possible with plain chocolate icing, the words, "A Touch of Momism" inscribed in white.

Discussions with submarine crews reveal that captains feel

differently about the degree of realism and frequency of drills, especially on patrol station. The consensus seems to be that the most competent and confident skippers do the most drilling, and that their crews feel the most competent and confident. Of course, sailors bitch about their training. Steam suits or anticontamination clothes are stifling, uncomfortable nuisances. Emergency Air Breathing masks (EABs) and Oxygen Breathing Apparatuses (OBAs) hinder movement and communication. In addition, the drills can eat into the movie schedule, but nobody can point to an instance when they canceled it. Old hands know it well—drills pay off!

Consider for one moment a situation in which a boat is operating under a thick spot in the polar ice cap, an area where breaking through may not be an option. What happens if a fire breaks out? It needn't be one that melts down a compartment, just one that erupts in a locker holding the patrol's supply of toilet paper, perhaps caused by a simple malfunction in the clothes dryer. Instantly the boat fills with noxious white smoke, and the carbon-monoxide level skyrockets as the paper smolders like some sort of punk. Two-thirds of the crew, asleep just after midnight, have to be aroused, and everyone dons an EAB, while the firefighters laboriously tear apart the paper and soak each smoldering roll. Once the fire is out, the emergency is far from over. The crew must wear the EABs for some four to six hours until the air-purification systems eliminate the deadly carbon monoxide, and special watches are set up to check on sleeping shipmates to assure they don't crimp the hoses of their life-sustaining air supply. And this is a *simple* fire, not oil, nor the oxygen system, nor the electrical connectors or switches of the storage battery or large generators.

▶

(Inset) Landing the DSRV *Mystic* on a mother sub. *(Lieutenant Cecil Davis, courtesy U.S. Navy)*

▶

USS *Pogy*, a nuclear attack submarine of the *Sturgeon* (SSN-637) class, rigged as a "mother sub," transports the Deep Submergence Rescue Vehicle (DSRV) to a practice area off San Diego. Operated by a skilled crew of three, the DSRV can locate disabled subs, land on them, transfer up to twenty-two people at a time, and return them to the submerged mother sub. Thrusters and ballasting systems make it possible for the DSRV to land on a sub with large lists or attitudes. Capable of operating down to 2,500 feet, the DSRV can be used under ice and can be transported by C-141 aircraft.

◀

Not things of beauty, but extremely functional, are the electrical, air, and water connections that serve the submarine during a busy maintenance period in a floating dry dock. Platforms, staging, and safety lines and nets assure the safety of workers high above the floor of the dock.

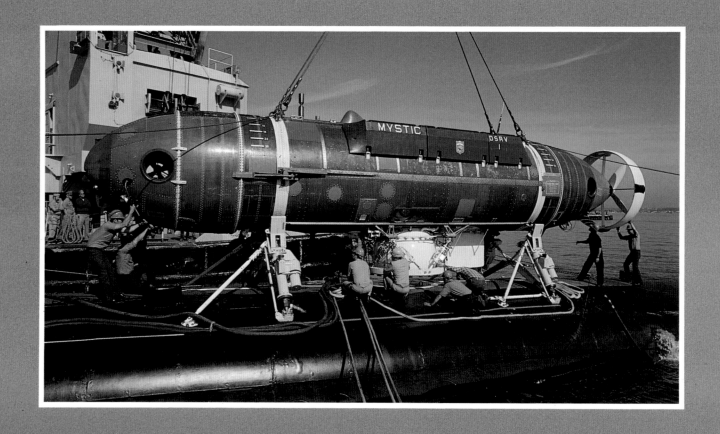

Throughout *Brooklyn,* the exactness of the orders and the precision with which each order is repeated are impressive. It appears that a captain can no longer reply simply, "Permission granted" to authorize a procedure that takes a requester several seconds or longer to spell out. Repetition occurs word by word, in some cases several times within the hearing of the man who will perform the act. As one veteran of many decades groused, "In the old days, the stress was on making the order simple, short, and direct. If the captain was in the head and said, 'Six-five feet!' the damned submarine itself would have made the depth 65 feet. The command didn't have to be acknowledged by such a string of watch standers in the same room." The order is no longer the simple and direct "Six-five feet" either, but a sentence: "Diving officer, make your depth six-five feet." It does seem cumbersome—not to mention time-consuming—to have the order pass through so many repetitions, and it is somewhat at odds with normal submarine efficiency and clarity.

The modern submariner makes another departure from the "Old Navy" ways by ignoring the circadian rhythm, the twenty-four-hour rotation of the earth upon which the body's functioning is based. For years most submarines used a schedule that called for four hours on watch and eight hours off, changing individual watch times only after a week to perhaps one-third of the trip. Thus the crew got accustomed to a routine. Today submariners are on watch for six long hours, followed by twelve hours off—a schedule that creates in effect an eighteen-hour day. Some men opine, "After two or three days, you feel like a zombie." Older submariners explain that six-hour watches were required when qualified watch standers were in short supply, in specific ratings, but that was for a six-on, six-off rotation—"port and starboard watches"—when the alternative would have allowed only four hours or less for rest. It was a schedule used only as long as it took new people to become qualified. However, the current schedule seems to be fairly acceptable to today's submariners.

With *Brooklyn's* transit to patrol station completed, the tempo doesn't seem to change much. Watches are stood, watches are relieved. Drills are conducted. But the boat now spends most of the time at periscope depth, using radio masts and sensors to detect any electronic emissions. The super-sensitive sonar is now listening all the time, and every ship in the vicinity is studied acoustically and electromagnetically. Radio reception is continuous, too, and world news is available. Experienced petty officers or officers quiz watch standers up for qualification, and these four-hour oral examinations echo the tempo of the patrol.

A good movie is shown daily, and often two on Sunday. On this boat there is a regular poker confederation that meets most evenings; however, the crew well recognizes that the Navy frowns upon gambling. Tournaments are scheduled for pinochle, cribbage, and acey-deucey. On Sundays the Mess Hall is rigged for church services, both Catholic and Protestant, with lay leaders selected from the crew. Nobody seems concerned about the noise of hymn singing; the airborne sounds of voices don't couple with the hull significantly. Some boats hold no drills on Sunday to create an identifiable break in the week, and other steps are taken to create the feeling that the pages of the calendar are turning. The routine is somewhat boring to some, but to most, up to their necks in learning a job and qualifying themselves or others, there just isn't enough time in the patrol.

The more ambitious members of *Brooklyn's* crew spend lots of time studying. Some take correspondence courses; one finds a quiet spot in a normally unoccupied space to set up his computer for a computer-driven course; another seeks the help of an officer in prepping for an exam for the Naval Academy. Some of the crewmen work out—running on treadmills, lifting weights, or doing calisthenics—but physical exercise is a pastime for only a few. The typical submariner is very well fed.

Brooklyn's crew is lucky to have another diversion, a clever cartoonist who captures the foibles of officers and sailors alike. Checking these sometimes irreverent portrayals, which are posted daily in the Mess Hall, is a habit of the skipper, who hopes that he is not the subject himself. A recent drawing showed seagulls landing atop the periscope on each observation, being roundly blessed by the skipper, and leaving behind some unpleasant blessings of their own.

Where is the tension, the anxiety of living in this potential tomb under tons of water? It simply doesn't seem to be there. The thought may occur to some that there is hazard in submarine duty, but few seem to dwell on what they feel very capable of handling. A serious casualty or problem will galvanize all hands to speedy action, of course. One young sailor has a practical attitude:"When you ride in an airliner, are you trembling and all shook up? No? We aren't either."

Each compartment of *Brooklyn* is fascinating. The Torpedo Room carries much more complex weapons than did submarines of old; the torpedoes today are really small subs, with their own highly capable sonar systems and brains. The Tomahawk missiles give the boat the capability to strike far inland, and the system for preparing and firing the missiles is the epitome of electronic genius, a portion of the BSY-1 (pronounced "Busy One") fire-control system. Noisemakers provide a means for breaking contact if an enemy is able to track the boat. A hydraulic loading and handling system shifts and loads all of these weapons. Today's torpedoman is a far cry from his 1945 counterpart. He is a practitioner not only of the mechanical, but also the electronic.

At the opposite end of the ship is the propeller shaft that drives the screw. Once the reactor and steam generators (a wordy description of what are essentially boilers) have produced the steam, the plant itself is not greatly different from those in older surface ships. The difference in a submarine, however, is the tremendous focus that has been placed on quietness of operation, reliability, and maintainability. However, since the steam plant has so much to do with the reactor, every watch stander must understand how what he does can influence reactor safety and the release of radiation. Each watch stander in the Maneuvering Room, for example, is expected to understand completely the interplay of his role with overall plant safety, to the degree that he can assume the duties of each of the others in an emergency, including those of the engineering officer of the watch.

The living spaces are luxurious for a warship. Comfortable bunks, with individual air-conditioning outlets and lights, also have curtains to provide a degree of privacy. A comfortable Mess Hall serves also as a place where the crew can relax with coffee and snacks at all hours, or where the men assemble for lectures and meetings. The Wardroom similarly serves the officers.

Somewhat taken for granted, but a feature that in its absence would greatly limit the capabilities of the modern submarine, is a safe, healthy atmosphere. In World War II subs, to say that the air was foul at the end of a seventeen-hour dive was to grossly understate. The fumes of diesel and lubricating oils filled the boats. The oxygen in the atmosphere, normally about 20 percent, hit the 17-percent level, while carbon dioxide built up to 3 percent from the crew's respiration. At this point, individuals experienced labored breathing or gasping, and even moving about became an effort. When used, a chemical absorbent filled the air with caustic dust. Smoking was often restricted, although the mere fact that the air would not support the lighting of matches made the restriction redundant. The foul odor of the sanitary collecting tanks, which required blowing to sea—and venting into the sub—did little to improve conditions. At the end of a long dive, headaches were commonplace. Little wonder that the first lieutenant, who was in charge of the ventilation and most other auxiliary systems, was known as "the officer in charge of stinks and leaks."

Even the clean clothing stowed in lockers became redolent of the heavy fuel fumes. One son of a submariner who bridged the era from diesel boats to the "nukes" recalls vividly the diesel odors that accompanied his father upon his return from even a day on his beloved boat. While esthetically unwelcome, the smell was not a total anathema. Because of the extra pay allotted to submariners, the characteristic aroma was also identified as "the green smell," or the "smell of money." To provide a controlled atmosphere, free of contaminants, marvelous carbon-dioxide scrubbers, oxygen generators, and the associated atmosphere-control equipment were invented, and these give *Brooklyn* the ability to remain submerged for months. Not a

development of the same magnitude as nuclear propulsion, perhaps, but a profound one nonetheless.

In the operations spaces both the sonar and fire-control equipments offer an amazing assortment of various colored lights, panels, and screens. It's a far cry from the look of the operations spaces during World War II, when the weaponry was limited to rather uncomplicated torpedoes, deck guns, and a torpedo-data computer. Today the weapons-systems officer's responsibility takes in a Disneyland array of torpedoes and missiles, a Tomahawk cruise missile capability from torpedo tubes as well as from twelve vertical launch tubes in the ballast tanks of the bow, evasion devices, the sonar systems, and the torpedo and missile fire-control systems, all rolled up in the BSY-1. The entry-level sailor assigned to weapons operation will have had two years of intensive training before he can even report to a submarine. For those accustomed to thinking of the engineer officer of a nuke as having the most exacting job, a hard look at the weapons area may show that such may no longer be the case. Each officer has plenty on his plate.

The people who maintain and operate all this super-sophisticated, and expensive, gear are all very young. The average age of the officers and enlisted men of the entire at-sea submarine force—counting the captains, commanders, and "old" chiefs—is 24.6 years.

Sonar is the heart of the sub's weapons suite, the driving factor in the bulk of submarine operations. This sensor has evolved from a rather simple listening device that, compared with today's wonders, might be viewed almost as a stethoscope compared with a CAT scan. With all of its sensitivity and flexibility, sonar would certainly play the major role in a naval war. The edge will go to the one who can make his boat least detectable, and to he who can shoot first. The careless will lose. A dropped wrench, the thoughtless clanging of a watertight door, a bad bearing in a motor or an imbalance in a rotor, a nicked propeller blade—any of these can provide a sustained or transient noise source that can draw a homing torpedo into a sub's vitals.

In a war of sound, the submarine may be likened to a battalion armed with its missiles and torpedoes, traversing a terrain of undersea canyons, hard or soft ocean bottoms that determine the echoing of sounds, and thermal layers that vary the vertical and horizontal structures of the ocean itself and can provide concealing curtains or, alternatively, channels acting as conduits for noises. The sonarman must understand fully the capabilities of the complex equipment he uses, but he must also recognize the unimportant noisemakers that clutter the sonar picture. In this type of warfare, the sonarmen are the "point men" for the battalion. This war, were it ever to be fought, would be one in which the warriors whisper.

A chief sonarman with years of experience in various types of boats describes the sonar capabilities of *Brooklyn's*

BSY-1 with obvious admiration: "We used to rely entirely on our hearing a target. Then we got recorders which used correlation techniques and made use of signals which the ear couldn't quite hear, printing it out or showing a deflection on a cathode-ray tube. Some of us felt like pinning our chiefs' crows on the damned machine. Now we've gone even further. Signal processing has advanced to where I feel we can just about pull signals out of the mud on the bottom! While we still depend a lot on ears, I'd have to say we're more dependent on the visual-presentation capability of this sucker. The gear can listen to a couple hundred beams, while a man can handle only one at a time. It's sensitive enough to pick up a minnow fart ten miles away. The only problem I have is making sure that the young kids don't get too complacent, yak too much, and goof off. In the next war a slight sniff may be all that you get."

With superb equipment, sensors, weaponry, and people at his call, the captain of the submarine, one might expect, can relax and let the well-trained crew perform. He does, but the degree of relaxation varies with the captain and the mission. Experience tells him that he must sustain the pressure, demanding innovative and meaningful training. Some skippers make a practice of touring the entire sub daily, some during some part of each section's watch each day, and some more and some less. Certainly the degree of attention paid by the skipper drives a crew's performance.

For those who speak or write of the loneliness of command, the submarine is probably not their model. In surface ships, the captain often is alone in his sea cabin near the Bridge, even eating alone or with one or two invited officers. Not so the submariner. Even a reserved skipper cannot escape the sharing of meals, conversation, and general camaraderie. Contact with others is unavoidable. And he should seek it out, for his business is his people.

On station, an uninterrupted sleep of more than several hours is rare for the submarine captain, and many get a good portion of their daily rest lying fully clothed, catching a few winks at random times.

The marvel of the BSY-1 with its plasma display is helpful. The captain can call up a menu of displays from his bunk or desk, some showing course, speed, and depth parameters, others depicting the position of the masts and antennas sticking above the top of the fairwater, the "sail" above the deck. Another valuable gadget is the "Periviz," a TV camera that when energized allows him to "tune in" on whatever the OOD is observing through the periscope. Alternatively, the crew can be privy to his own observations and watch the show from several locations, either as it is occurring or later on tape. Undoubtedly, the device, if available, would have reduced the claimed tonnage of World War II sinkings.

Some skippers cut down on the interruptions of the night by having the exec serve as a command duty officer—supervising the watches, receiving reports, and notifying the captain only when necessary. In some cases the exec might operate the boat, always within some sort of bounds set by the skipper. Other skippers—some with unbounded ability and stamina, some who have not built up the trust in an alter ego, or some who are super-cautious—take on the entire load at all times. After all, the accountability of the commanding officer is absolute: whatever happens to the boat, the fault or the credit is his. If an officer entrusted with a specific duty fails, it is the captain's training or supervision of the officer that can be faulted, or his judgment of the person's ability. It is his world for the few years he holds command. Naval officers savor the opportunity to command any ship, but especially those who train for a war in which warriors whisper—the submariners.

Stealth personified, USS *Cavalla* operates at periscope depth while working with SEAL teams. Swimmers are able to "lock out" of subs, working with rubber boats stowed in topside lockers, or with a swimmer-delivery vehicle carried in topside hangars, and may ride a small submersible to perform their operation. *(U.S. Navy)* ▶ ▶▶

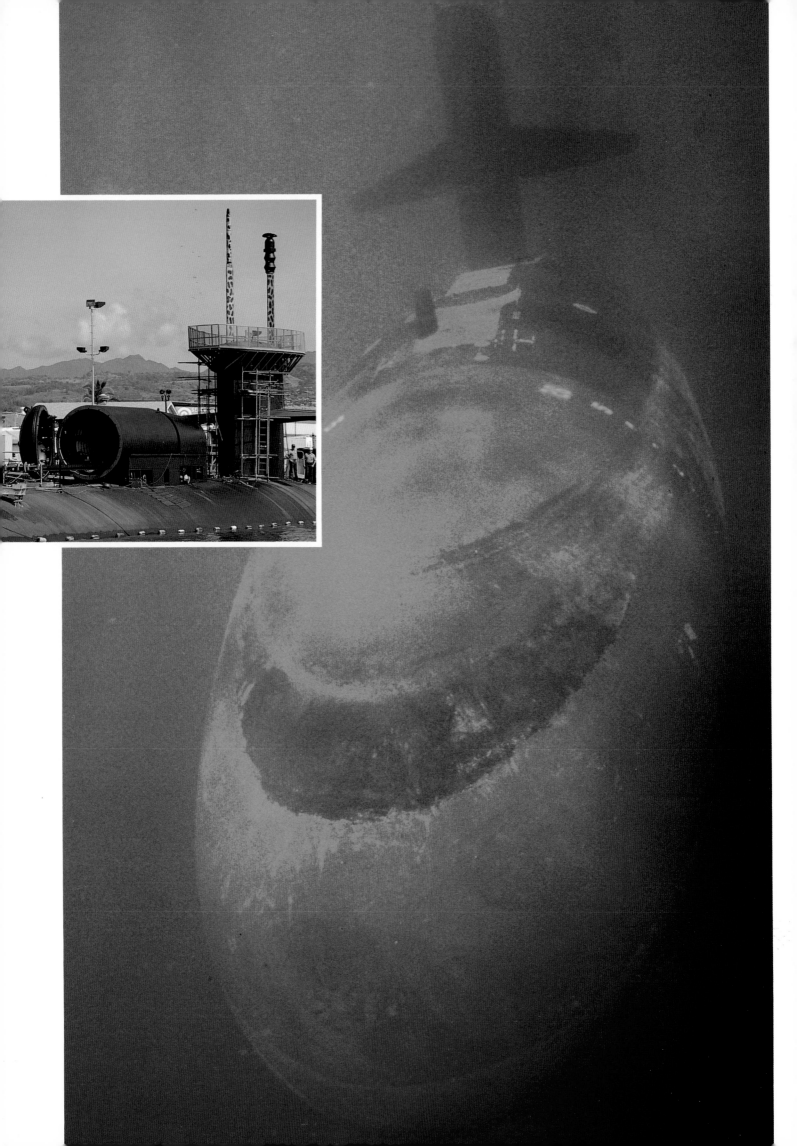

▲

The captain and Bridge watch of *City of Corpus Christi* as she transits to her diving point at maximum speed.

◄

(Inset) At pierside in Pearl Harbor, Hawaii, USS *William H. Bates* is fitted with a stowage container for a swimmer-delivery vehicle.

◄

Operating submerged in an area of the ocean's clearest waters, *Cavalla* is an example of the protective curtain that assures the stealth aspects of submarines. *(U.S. Navy)*

An Elizabeth River pilot joins the captain on the Bridge of *Jefferson City* as she makes her way back to Norfolk, Virginia.

Conducting special operations near the North Pole, USS *Trepang* surfaces through the ice. *(U.S. Navy)*

USS *Archerfish* departs the base at La Maddalena, Italy. With a deployed submarine-squadron commander and staff, this base provides command and logistics for American submarines deployed to the Mediterranean Sea.

On a beautiful and typical Hawaiian day, the crew of USS *San Francisco* loads provisions the old-fashioned way, and the hard way, hand by hand, piece by piece, through restricting 30-inch hatches and down vertical ladders.

◀

One of the newest attack subs, USS *Jefferson City* transits the shipping lanes off Norfolk en route to her diving point.

▲

With an eye to the fried chicken while hot rolls await the oven, the cook on board USS *Narwhal* prepares the noon meal.

▲

The captain and officers of *Jacksonville* enjoy a lively conversation and recount their experiences over dinner in the wardroom.

▲

In the crew's washroom area, resplendent with shining, corro-sion-resistant steel, a crew member of USS *Jacksonville* per-forms the daily scrape off of whiskers. In days past, this and other matters of personal hygiene husbanded scarce fresh water—not the case in today's submarine Navy, where fresh water is plentiful.

For many captains, the at-sea position of the bunk is down—as a bunk—forsaking the in-port bureaucratic desk and paper-work. Catching sleep between reports and evolutions is an art. Catnaps are a necessity, inevitably to be interrupted by the ringing of the phone next to his bunk. He must receive reports on a variety of situations or conditions because all are ulti-mately his responsibility. Seen here, a dozing captain in USS *Albany,* one of the first of the Improved 688 class of attack subs.

▶

In the chief petty offi-
cers' quarters of
Topeka, the chief of the
boat talks with his
shipmates. The photo
of a *Topeka* hero behind
him contrasts markedly
with the popular pin-
ups in the sailors' quar-
ters.

▲

The crew of *Jacksonville*, which is operating out of Norfolk, Virginia, fills the tables of the crew's mess hall with a variety of spirited card games.

In the crew's bunking areas, some men like privacy, some don't care. Reading is popular, and heading for one's "rack" gets one away from the rubbing of shoulders and hips in the passageways or the conversations in the mess hall. ▶▶

◀

Space is always at a premium, even in the largest subs. In USS *Atlanta* a young sailor finds a small nook in which to set up his computer and complete a correspondence course with self-teaching videocassettes.

▲

The captain of USS *Topeka* receives a last-minute report of readiness for getting underway as he checks on items of work completed. The captain's stateroom has all the creature comforts—one just has to know how to rig them. The bunk folds up to stow flush into the bulkhead. A desk folds down from underneath the bunk. A fold-down basin is installed, and just outside the stateroom is a head (toilet) and shower, shared with the executive officer. A number of indicators are installed to provide information on the boat's course, speed, and depth, and in the latest class of subs a plasma display provides a menu of options for the captain, such as an indication of the position of all masts and periscopes. Also provided is a television repeater that shows whatever the officer of the deck is looking at with the periscope, if desired.

▲

Jefferson City is distinctive without fairwater planes on the sail, making her way out of the Elizabeth River en route to the Virginia Capes Operating Area.

USS *Salt Lake City* demonstrates her top speed while heading out to her diving area. ▶

▲

The diving officer and planesmen control the depth and angle
of the highly maneuverable *Skipjack. Skipjack,* no longer in
commission, was the first nuclear attack submarine to be
designed with a totally round cross section—the hull previously tested in the diesel submarine *Albacore.* The design also
initiated the use of a single propeller. The combination provided in *Skipjack* a submarine so fast and maneuverable that
those operating it likened the experience to flying a fighter aircraft. However, unlike a jet, fast turns in that sub did not produce stabilizing "G forces." Consequently, the sound of an
entire setting of chinaware crashing to the decks was heard
with disturbing frequency.

▲

An integral part of the advanced BSY-1 fire-control system, the sonar installation of USS *Topeka* is "top of the line," able to perform remarkable tasks compared with even the installations of subs only several years older. Here, sonar operators rely more and more on visual indications rather than the aural capability used by a past generation, and the equipment makes possible the scanning of hundreds of beams simultaneously, a feat not approachable with human ears.

◀

On board USS *Albany,* recently developed "plasma display" presentations make possible the calling up of a menu of displays simply by touching the screen with a finger. The captain's stateroom also has a repeater. Seen here is the display that shows the position of each mast and periscope that extend from the sail.

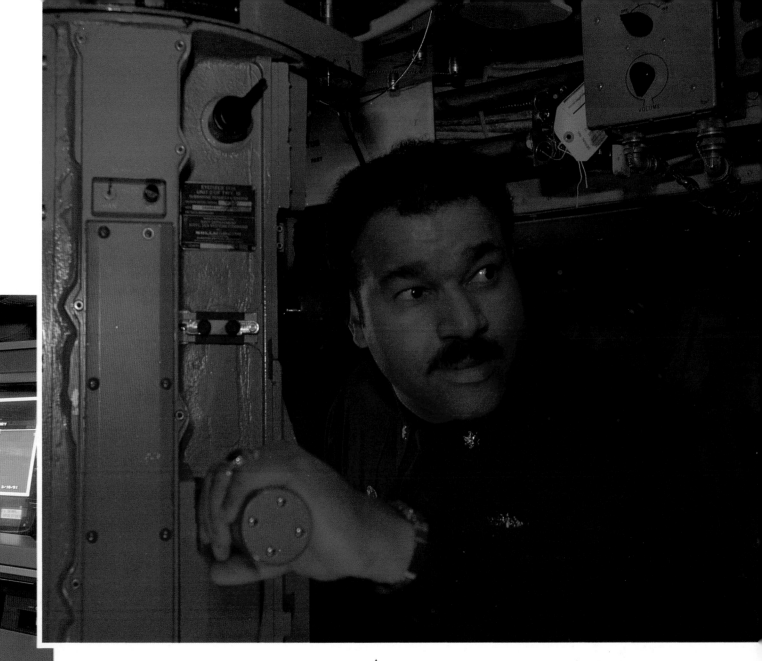

▲

The captain of USS *Jacksonville* checks targets with the periscope. The boat is rigged for red lighting so that the watch standers' eyes can adapt to darkness.

◀

A *Los Angeles*–class submarine of the Improved-688 class, USS *Albany* sports a new and highly capable fire-control system, the BSY-1, called "Busy One" by her crew. The system completely integrates the computers for Tomahawk missiles, torpedoes, sonars, and indications for the captain's stateroom, with those for tracking targets and deriving fire-control solutions, i.e., the course and speed of targets. Seen here—aside from the complex of fire-control panels with, in this case, a map of the East Coast of the U.S.—is a screen that can, on call, display the noise signatures from a library of targets, while the screen in the center is a television repeater of what is being seen by the periscope at the time.

▲

As a demonstration of her ability to "go where no man has gone before," *Nautilus* became the first submarine ever to steam beneath the ice at the North Pole on 3 August 1958. Artist Peter W. Rogers takes us beneath the submarine for an unusual perspective, looking up toward the ice. Altogether *Nautilus* was under the arctic ice for ninety-six hours and a total of 1,830 miles. Her skipper at the time, Commander William R. Anderson, told of the ship's epic voyage in a book titled *Nautilus Ninety North*, indicating the latitude reached for the first time by undersea voyagers. Once the submarine returned to civilization, she made a triumphant voyage to New York City, and her crew was feted in a parade up Fifth Avenue. *(Submarine Force Library and Museum)*

◀

USS *Buffalo* leaps from the depths off Pearl Harbor in a 1988 test of its emergency-blow capability, to verify the sub's ability to surface rapidly. This blowing of ballast tanks with very high pressure air, coupled with use of speed and "up angles," is one of several safety procedures recommended by investigators after the loss of *Thresher* in 1963.

A torpedoman in *Salt Lake City* loosens the restraining straps
holding a torpedo in place, prior to loading the tube.

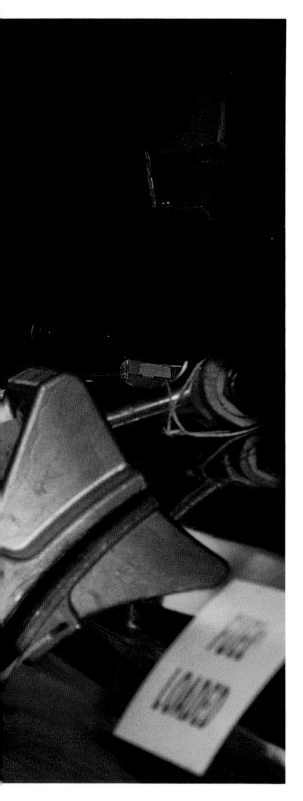

▲

In her home port of San Diego, *Haddock*, a 594-class attack submarine, loads exercise Mark 48 torpedoes. The brightly painted exercise torpedoes are easily spotted during recovery. This class of subs is unique in requiring the torpedoes to be loaded vertically. Earlier and later classes used the angled method, in which a skid is slanted down into the torpedo room and the 3,000-pound weapon is eased down by sailors with snubbing tending lines.

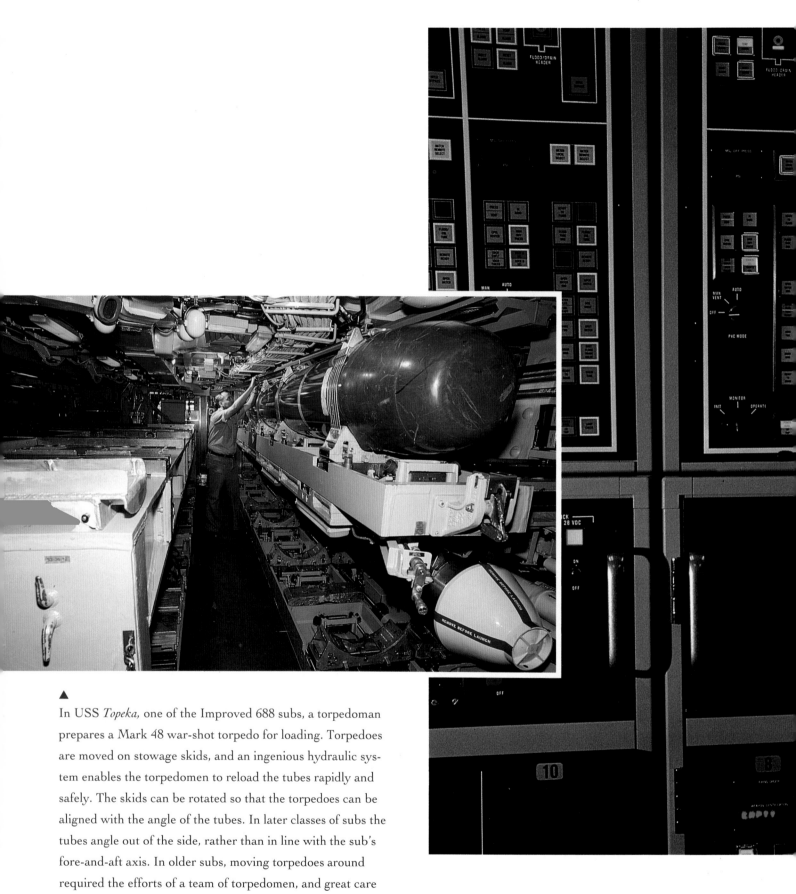

In USS *Topeka*, one of the Improved 688 subs, a torpedoman prepares a Mark 48 war-shot torpedo for loading. Torpedoes are moved on stowage skids, and an ingenious hydraulic system enables the torpedomen to reload the tubes rapidly and safely. The skids can be rotated so that the torpedoes can be aligned with the angle of the tubes. In later classes of subs the tubes angle out of the side, rather than in line with the sub's fore-and-aft axis. In older subs, moving torpedoes around required the efforts of a team of torpedomen, and great care had to be taken not to let the boat take angles or rolls for fear that the 3,000-pound weapons would crush someone. Modern subs may be required to pull out torpedoes and shift loads rapidly because there are so many different types of weapons or devices in use.

▲

The high-tech Vertical Launch System (VLS) panels in the
torpedo room, a portion of the BSY-1 system, contrasts with
an emblem from the "Old Navy," the fancy tattoo. Here the
young torpedoman, on board *Topeka*, checks out the Tomahawk panels prior to approving the recently loaded missiles.

▲

In the torpedo room of USS *Salt Lake City*, a torpedoman monitors the settings on the torpedo-readiness panel preparatory to firing.

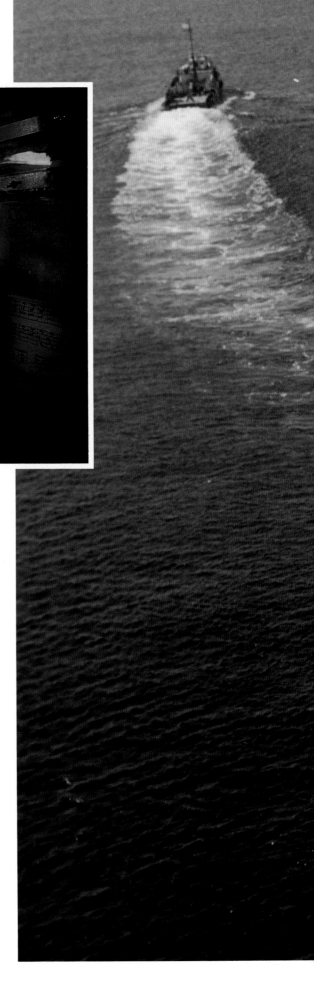

In the early 1960s the Beatles entertained us by singing, "We all live in a yellow submarine." Then the song spawned a movie, and then life imitated art. In 1976 a tugboat towed the former USS *Menhaden*, originally commissioned in 1945, to Keyport, Washington. There she served as a target, both surfaced and submerged, for the testing of torpedoes, to acquire data on their effectiveness. She was painted yellow to facilitate damage assessment. The letters on her sail, NUSC, stand for the organization that sponsored the tests, the Naval Undersea Systems Center. *(National Archives, 428-KN-25569)* ▶

Early dawn at the submarine base in San Diego reveals the *Los Angeles*–class attack subs *La Jolla* (left) and *Salt Lake City* in port for maintenance. ▶▶

▲

USS *Haddock* departs her home port of San Diego for the "bone-yard" in the Pacific, the repository for decommissioned ships, signaling the final chapter of the 594-class subs in the Pacific.

◀

A panorama of the submarine base at San Diego reveals that the base is busy, with two attack-submarine tenders. Also represented is each class of the most modern submarines. The newest *Los Angeles* class is closest. Farther out lies the smaller sail of the SSN-594 class and the larger SSN-637 class.

▲

U.S. Naval Academy and NROTC midshipmen are transferred by tugs to operational nuclear submarines for several days under the ocean as part of their indoctrination during summer-cruise period.

▲
One of the newest of the Improved 688 class (688-I), USS *Jefferson City* exercises the muzzle doors of the twelve Vertical Launch System (VLS) tubes. In a marvelous adaptation of the 688-class boats, one that demonstrates the wisdom of providing room for growth in basic submarine designs, vertical tubes were installed in the forward ballast tanks of submarines under construction, commencing with hull number 751 (*Jefferson City* is number 759). Tomahawk missiles are loaded vertically, using specialized loading adapters. The missiles are given a final preparation and checkout prior to the boat's going to sea and then remain in their tubes for the duration of the patrol. There is no capability to repair any defects in the missiles themselves. *Topeka* and *Pittsburgh* demonstrated the efficacy of this design and the reliability of Tomahawk in Desert Storm.

In the torpedo room of the VLS-equipped *Albany*, a torpedoman checks all systems on the Tomahawk firing panels of the BSY-1 fire-control system. Today's torpedomen must be a mixture of electronic technician and mechanic. ▶

◀

USS *Louisville* is seen here returning to her home port of San Diego, California. A sub of the 688-I, or "improved *Los Angeles*," class of attack submarines, the ship has a Vertical Launch System (VLS) installation of twelve external tubes holding Tomahawk missiles. *Louisville* was the first sub to shoot Tomahawks in the Gulf war in 1991, joined shortly after by *Pittsburgh*. The great flexibility and endurance of the class are evident in this account by her captain, Commander Frank Stewart: "*Louisville* departed San Diego on 27 December 1990 en route to Operation Desert Shield.... high speed transit to the northern Red Sea commenced.... across the Pacific Ocean, through the South Pacific islands and across the Indian Ocean.... USS *Louisville* fired the first shot in anger from a US submarine since World War II ... on January 19, 1991 when *Louisville* conducted a Tomahawk strike against an Iraqi target.... *Louisville* had transited further faster than any previous ship of any type in any navy...." The sub then returned to Guam at high speed for a missile reload and returned to the Red Sea at high speed. When *Louisville* returned to San Diego on 29 April 1991, there was a warm and spectacular homecoming, which included the presentation of a special-edition "Louisville Slugger" baseball bat to each member of the crew.

USS *Salt Lake City* returns to her home port of San Diego in heavy fog, virtually a portrait of stealth. ▶

A chief torpedoman supervises the checkout of Tomahawk missiles just loaded on board *Topeka* in San Diego. With twelve vertical launch tubes loaded with Tomahawks, and a capability for stowing and firing additional missiles for the four torpedo tubes as well as torpedoes, a single submarine becomes a very potent addition to a force of warships or is capable of striking fixed targets discreetly and independently.

▲

Submerged in the Pacific Ocean, an attack submarine has in recent minutes fired a test Tomahawk missile. When it arrives over land, a complex system takes over the missile's navigation, matching radar profiles of the terrain with those that were previously stored into its memory. On-board computers adjust the missile's course, and the Tomahawk may be programmed to approach targets on a variety of bearings, avoiding defenses or using the radar shadows provided by hills and valleys. The missile's destructive power and virtually perfect accuracy are evident in this firing on the San Clemente Island range, where the Tomahawk explodes exactly over a bunkered aircraft. *(U.S. Navy)*

Women and children rush to greet husbands, fathers, and sweethearts upon the return of USS *Honolulu* to Pearl Harbor, Hawaii, after a six-month deployment. ▶

◄

The captain of USS *Honolulu* greets his wife and children upon returning from a six-month deployment.

▲

A sad occasion for present and past members of the crew of USS *Scamp* is the colorful decommissioning ceremony at Submarine Base Bangor, Washington. Some thirty of *Scamp*'s original commissioning crew came from far and near, recounting the thrills and frustrations they had known during their time on board. One memorable incident occurred during the boat's initial sea trials: the propeller shaft broke off, and the propeller was lost. Ignominiously, the boat had to be towed to the shipyard at Mare Island, California. Fortunately, the fracture occurred just outside the rear cone of the hull; had it been several feet forward, the ship would almost certainly have been lost. In this ceremony, a watch section of sailors departs ship, one by one, until the last has crossed the brow, or gangplank, for the last time.

Boomers

DETERRENCE FROM THE DEEP

n this post–Cold War era, it may be difficult to recall the degree of international tension and suspicion that marked the rivalry between the United States and the Soviet Union. A whole generation has passed since children went through "duck-and-cover" drills—hiding under a desk or other piece of furniture and covering their heads, to practice what they would do if a nuclear weapon hit their nation. Who remembers community and individual bomb shelters, stocked with provisions? Who has heard the sirens announcing practice air-raid alerts? Who still fears the scenario depicted in the popular movie *On the Beach,* in which a nuclear shoot-out has so filled the world with radiation that death is inevitable?

America's leaders concluded that deterring a nuclear war made a lot more sense than did the bomb shelters and air-raid drills, which would deal with the effects of an attack, not prevent it. The idea of deterrence through a policy of "massive retaliation" came into being in the 1950s: the United States would so impress the Soviet Union with our ability to wage nuclear war that Soviet leaders would be foolish to start anything. At first the existing manned bombers of the Strategic Air Command were to deliver retaliatory attacks. Later, intercontinental ballistic missiles were added to the force. Soon, under an aggressive Chief of Naval Operations, Admiral Arleigh Burke, the Navy began to develop its own contribution to the strategic-deterrent "mix." The submarine was the obvious choice for the ballistic-missile platform because of its inherent stealth and survivability. After all, you can't hit what you can't see, or what you can't hear.

Of course, the advantages of the new Polaris system were not lost on the rest of the world. In rapid order the Soviet Union, the United Kingdom, France, and China virtually copied the concept. Predictably, the Soviet Navy proceeded to surpass the United States, building a numerically superior force of diesel- and nuclear-powered submarines. When the U.S. Navy introduced the huge Trident submarine, the Soviets apparently saw its great size as a challenge and answered with their own leviathan, the huge Typhoon. But Polaris set the pattern.

"Cut 'Scorpion' in half and add a missile compartment!" was the solution put forth in 1958 to hurry things along. "Scorpion" was the intended name, but the ship on the building ways at Electric Boat Company would soon be launched as *George Washington,* the first Polaris submarine. With only a few cruise-missile subs at sea in 1957, the United States was playing "catch-up." The Soviets had launched Sputnik, the first artificial Earth satellite, and already had nuclear-armed ballistic missiles at sea in converted Zulu-class submarines. The Polaris program, undoubtedly the most successful weapons-development program ever undertaken, was run by Rear Admiral William F. "Red" Raborn, a naval aviator, with the help of Captain Levering Smith as the project's technical director.

Even though the development of Polaris required a succession of minor technical miracles, the concept for the deterrent force was quite simple. The Navy would rotate a series of missile submarines on patrol, thus ensuring it always had boats on station, ready on short notice to deliver an effective retaliatory nuclear attack. Submarines would have an advantage over manned bombers in that they wouldn't have to penetrate enemy air space, and they had an advantage over land-based missiles in that their launching sites, being unknown and undetectable, couldn't be targeted in advance.

Keeping these new ships at sea a maximum percentage of their operational lives required a revolutionary maintenance concept, a dedicated supply system, and two-crew manning (dubbed "Blue" and "Gold"), all of which would permit a fast turnaround of the sub after each patrol and make maximum use of the expensive assets. The two-crew system would be good for the submariners too. While the Blue crew, for example, was at sea for a long patrol, the members of the Gold crew would be able to receive training ashore, attend to administrative work, and spend some time on leave with their families—

◀

Trident submarine USS *Georgia* runs at high power in Straits of Juan de Fuca, Washington, enroute dive point to start deterrent patrol in the Pacific.

somewhat like most other human beings. This scheme is still at the heart of the deterrent force today.

The earliest Polaris missiles had ranges of approximately twelve hundred and fifteen hundred miles, far longer than their early Soviet submarine counterparts. Nevertheless, the original concept featured overseas bases in Scotland, Spain, and Guam so that the transit to and from the United States wouldn't diminish the time the subs could spend within effective missile range of the targets. The increased range of later Polaris and Poseidon models, and finally the present Trident, meant that overseas basing was no longer necessary. Following the departure of the tender and her brood from Holy Loch, Scotland, in early 1992, all basing for the large missile boats is now within the continental United States.

As the Polaris subs reach the end of their careers, they are being replaced by the much more effective and quieter Trident submarines. Roughly twice the tonnage of previous SSBNs, with a submerged displacement even greater than that of the *Baltimore*-class cruisers of World War II vintage, the Trident submarine is 560 feet long—almost two football fields—with a hull diameter of 42 feet. Trident was criticized for its size during lengthy congressional hearings and by adversary groups intent upon killing the large submarine program.

The huge Trident made possible improvements in many areas, not the least of which was quietness. Opponents were vociferous in claiming that the sub would be vulnerable because of noise. In response to congressional questioning on this issue, a lead Navy witness testified to a number of possible quieting measures, adding, "Sir, if we achieve our established design goal for noise, the enemy will have to shoot at the quiet spot in the ocean—not the noisy one!" Trident designers and engineers not only achieved but exceeded that goal. Detection of Trident is a challenge to the best of SSNs, which might even bump into her before knowing she was there.

While it may sound strange, perhaps it is the time in port that is most critical to the success of Trident, as well as of other subs. A boat coming off patrol has a planned schedule of tests and evolutions to complete. Certain items are programmed for replacement, with packages containing the necessary parts having been assembled and provided to base workers beforehand. Six-foot logistic hatches are opened, three per ship; these are much more accommodating than the 26- or 30-inch hatches of earlier subs. Trying to construct and repair those earlier boats was akin to building a ship in a bottle, and loading them with a ninety-day supply of provisions—dry, fresh, and frozen foods—was a two day, all-hands chore. A few men and women can put these same supplies aboard Trident in three hours. Both of Trident's two crews work around the clock to accomplish maintenance during the short refit period. Dependents live on the base, so there is no "crew flight" to distant bases, as happened with the earlier SSBNs. All of this hard work and team effort assures the continued effectiveness and morale of the crew, and the availability of the boats.

Ask any SSBN captain his primary mission on patrol, and he will answer, "Remain undetected." Later he may mention maintaining communications reception, keeping missiles in range and ready for firing, or some other aspect of his submarine's purpose. But he will steadfastly stress as the absolutely inviolate first priority the stealth that sets his system apart from all other deterrents. Any enemy will know, realizing that you can't stop what you can't see or hear, that retaliation to any attack on the United States is inevitable.

The patrol routine for "boomers"—a long-standing nickname for the large missile boats—is not greatly different from that of attack submarines, except that the missile subs don't chance detection and normally don't approach contacts to investigate their business. Boomer skippers must aggressively train their crews in emergency procedures and casualty repairs. In addition, the men are called upon several times each patrol to perform a countdown and simulated missile launch. The skipper's primary concern, of course, is to be able to launch missiles on assigned targets should the President so order. The skipper and his officers frequently rehearse the steps necessary to assure this capability. "What if... ?" provides much food for discussion.

A Polaris or Trident patrol is an exercise in patience and skillful leadership for a skipper. He must use imagination to keep up his crew's alertness in many patrol areas, which may be devoid of contacts. Many captains, in fact, look forward to times when hundreds of fishing vessels blanket a boat's assigned sector. Their presence raises a crew's attention level and provides maneuvering practice to conning officers as they avoid fishing trawls and trawlers. In some areas there is always the possibility of competition, a non-U.S. submarine. Some captains worry about this, others relish the experience. It provides the best peacetime opportunity to gather information that may be needed in potential future hostilities.

Let's join a hypothetical Trident submarine, USS *Hawaii,* on patrol in the Pacific. She steams on random courses as she carries out her deterrent patrol in a generally less hostile environment than the stormy North Atlantic, which has been the location for the bulk of patrols since *George Washington* first went to sea. No person knows in advance the courses *Hawaii* takes, or when she may take them. Sometimes a random roll of the dice may determine her heading. And no person not on the boat at that moment knows within many miles just where she is. Some might liken the sub's extreme silence and purposeful movements to the stealthy slinking of a cat, or the gliding of an owl, or even the slithering of an earthworm.

In the middle of the night two-thirds of the crew is sleeping. *Hawaii*'s cooks and baker have just toasted the new day with pineapple juice. Suddenly, the peace is shattered by the "gonging" of the General Alarm. The bread dough is left to rise for itself.

An incoming message had brought the captain to instant alertness, and his announcement, "Battle Stations, Missile" moves the men quickly but quietly to their positions.

Compressed air hisses as the pressure in the missile tubes is equalized with sea pressure to permit the muzzle doors to open. Two-man teams of officers check and recheck the authorizing orders that would emanate from the President of the United States. Other two-officer teams twirl the dials on the double-combination safes to gain access to other items essential to missile launch. Sonars search for any trace of an enemy, and torpedo fire-control systems are placed in readiness to respond to a surprise attack. The noise of a launch would allow any nearby opposition submarine to detect *Hawaii*.

On the diving controls, surrounded by a kaleidoscope of colored indicator lights, the diving officer ballasts the sub carefully as she slows to a stop, maintaining the ordered depth within a foot or so. Planesmen move the control surfaces to counter each bobble caused by wave action. Soon the diving officer transfers the task of holding the ordered depth to an electronic hovering system. It's a sensitive system that alternately expels water ballast from a huge tank as the sub gains weight or admits water into another tank if the sub gets light. In the Control Room the gasps of air resemble the labored breathing of a giant whale.

In the Missile Control Center, several technicians monitor a Christmas tree of dancing, flashing lights—now red, now amber, now green—incomprehensible to any but the most trained. In all parts of the boat the officers and men go through checklist after checklist to make *Hawaii* and her twenty-four missiles fully ready. It has been only a few minutes since the receipt of the launch message. The captain places the final key into a panel at the periscope station, and a missile technician holds a firing key that will complete the circuits firing gas generators to send the missiles skyward. When the launch circuits are completed, there will be a muffled "whoosh," and the giant sub will bounce and her stern section whip a bit from the great forces driving a heavy missile skyward from the tube. Jolt will follow jolt only a few seconds apart until all the assigned missiles are fired.

But there will be no jolts from launches this day. Thankfully, this evolution, as in all other similar ones in the world's great navies, has been an exercise. Such no-notice readiness drills occur regularly. Perhaps it is precisely because of the credibility of these undersea deterrent forces that they have never had to be used in earnest. For decades force has faced force, not in the classic sense of tanks battling tanks or warships firing salvos at warships, but invisibly and distantly, attesting to the inevitability of massive destruction should the politicians of this planet miscalculate.

• • •

Over the years, as technology has enabled, submarines have become larger and larger to accommodate equipment that gives them the capability to carry out additional missions. But there is evidence that the growth of these leviathans was about to cease even before the breaking out of peace in recent years.

For certain, in assessing the potential vulnerabilities of the total strategic deterrent system, U.S. planners had been contemplating placing fewer nuclear missiles on each boomer. The United Kingdom and France apparently were not persuaded to go beyond the classic sixteen-tube Polaris configuration, and the former Soviet Union, having succeeded in building a giant in the twenty-missile Typhoon, apparently terminated the series at six but was continuing the smaller Delta-IV class at the time of the breakup of the USSR.

What of the Typhoon? Do pronouncements of less frequent strategic-missile patrols and the announced dismantling of, perhaps significantly, six submarines signify that the model will have only a brief lifetime? Will she eventually prove to have been the ultimate in construction of large submarines? She is a giant indeed. Typhoon is an anglicized version of the Russian name "Taifun," which means shark, and this is the largest of the sharks of steel.

Only recently have accounts of the Typhoon's living conditions and operating capabilities become available. One of this book's coauthors, himself a submariner, was permitted by the Soviet Minister of Defense to visit several bases, training facilities, and submarines just prior to the now-historic coup attempt in August 1991. The icing on the cake of his tour was a stop on board a Typhoon in the Northern Fleet headquarters port of Severomorsk. His photographs and an accompanying film crew's videotapes depict the boat's great size, explore her interior spaces, and show her leaving port, diving, and surfacing. All of these hitherto-hidden scenes of the Typhoon have since been a source of wonder and amazement to audiences of U.S. submariners.

Arriving at the pier, the startled visitor gapes at the giant and exclaims, "That's not a submarine; it's a goddamn mountain!" The translation of his reaction into Russian brings howls of laughter from the hosts. The massive shape, with much, much reserve buoyancy, towers above the pier. Almost twice the width of the large Trident, and about the same length, this sub displaces a third again the tonnage—twenty-five thousand tons—and carries a payload of twenty ballistic missiles. Her solid construction is impressive, as is the amount of sound-absorbing coating spread over the entire hull and inside the great sail. The high, thick rudder towers above those standing on the after deck—a riveting sight.

The visitor is welcomed by a group of officers on the large deck, each wearing a neat set of bright blue coveralls that bear in Cyrillic letters the name or the primary duty of the individual. Several officers are hoisting the naval colors, and the blue of their uniforms and of the clear Arctic sky contrasts sharply with the bright reds of the ensign and jack of that pre-coup period and of the flask, resembling a canteen, that each submariner wears over his shoulder or on his belt. This flask contains a face mask and an individual supply of a chemical that when energized will provide the wearer with a ten-minute supply of oxygen. Clearly, there is a concern for safety.

The skipper, Captain (First Rank) Andrej Zhygilev, is the son of an admiral. He speaks a fair English and is a friendly and accommodating host. Thirty-nine years old, he has been in command of this submarine for three years and anticipates two more years on board. His experience has not included a variety of submarines, as is usual in other countries, but has been exclusively in nuclear-missile subs. The videotape records his pride and sense of humor at the exchange of gifts—caps, insignia, books—including, from the American, some packs of chewing gum bearing the prominent and colorful trade name Trident.

In the compartments that could be filmed, a tip of the hat to the habitability standards of U.S. nuclear subs is obvious. The crew's berthing is comparable to modern U.S. standards, far removed from that of the earlier Foxtrot, Kilo, and Juliett diesels or even of U.S. diesels. Rather than a crew's Mess Hall and officers' Wardroom, one very large communal Mess Hall serves officers and enlisted men together. Captain Zhygilev heads one table with several senior officers but also with sailors intermixed. The sailors enjoy small glasses of white wine, but there is no alcohol for the officers. Orange salmon caviar is available, spread on good black bread. Throughout the meal the crew listens to raucous music, not at all unfamiliar to young people in the United States. Running on the large TV is a "Tom and Jerry" cartoon, its music playing snatches of "Jingle Bells." Obviously Captain Zhygilev does not suffer indigestion from the clamor, or else he is showing U.S. visitors that "if you can take it, we can."

About 50 officers are included in the Typhoon's total crew of about 150. This is a very high ratio compared with that of her U.S. counterparts, but the officers' ranks include a number of "michmen," or warrant officers. Unlike U.S. officers, Soviet officers stand watches only in their areas of specialization. A captain (second rank), equivalent to a U.S. commander, explains that he is a computer officer and that he stands watches in turn with other officers of the same grade and specialty. He never stands watches as officer of the deck, diving officer, or engineering officer of the watch.

This officer also explains the reason for the apparently high quality of the food and living conditions on board Typhoon and for the crew's dependents who live in the far north. The provisioning of submarine sailors in the Northern Fleet is better than that of their counterparts elsewhere to compensate for the hardships of the climate and location, where winter nights are twenty-four hours long. In the boat's messing area are an aquarium and an aviary in which several colorful finches chirp. The visitor's jibe, "Is that your carbon-monoxide detector?" brings uninhibited laughter. A young officer smiles in wonder and comments, "We didn't think that an American flag officer would have such a sense of humor."

There is a recreational space whose bulkheads are painted with pastoral or wooded scenes. Several sailors and officers move slowly in rocking chairs. A guitar player strums and softly sings a song of the country while his shipmates read. In the mini-arcade, other sailors are engrossed in computer video games. A shipboard gymnasium allows rowing, weight lifting, running on treadmills, and calisthenics. Few of the young sailors appear overweight. In recognition of the tobacco habit, which seems more prevalent than in the United States, a small smoking compartment is set aside, sealed off from the rest of the boat. Then comes the unbelievable: a sauna seating perhaps a half dozen perspiring and smiling sailors, and a hot tub that must require "zero bubble" dives, that is, flat, with no angle, to avoid spilling the water into the boat.

Despite the great attention paid to streamlining the hull and to applying sound-absorbing and sound-damping coatings, much of the top of the bridge, unlike that of its U.S. counterparts, is free-flooding, with no clamshell cover to guard against flow noise and eddies. In contrast, several installations farther aft on the sail are provided with such fairing. Apparently, the designers were concerned with quietness only at very slow speed, so the design is consistent with the manner in which the sub is operated under the ice.

Typhoon's controls appear well-automated, with planesmen and helmsman operating knob-type controls rather than the wheel or joystick customary in other subs. The periscope is large and obviously contains more than simply optical devices. Diving, though, is an unusually slow and time-consuming operation, probably because of the large amount of positive buoyancy and the absence of vent valves in the main deck. The long dive really is more a "controlled sinking," but that is not a criticism. There is little operational need for fast dives in modern nuclear submarines, particularly for those that operate beneath the ice. The captain comments that the Russian submarine design stresses survivability, another clue to her high-riding posture when on the surface. This concern, the captain continues, explains the television camera mounted on the main deck aft—he uses it to judge the makeup of the ice. Then he shows the effects of recent under-ice operations: new patches in the coating on top of the massive rudder and fractures of the tiles on the forward top of the Bridge.

The American visitor is impressed at the formality and discipline evident in the crew's evolutions, much as he had been earlier when observing the performance of Soviet trainees and diesel-submarine crews. One thing is clear—these submariners of the far north are as proud of their status as submariners, and of the things that set them apart from the sailors of other warships, as are their American counterparts. They express repeatedly their feeling that submariners are brothers of a sort, regardless of language or location.

Having seen the capabilities of this largest of the behemoths, we can contemplate her use. The following scenario may be representative.

At the top of the Earth lies the polar cap—a flat expanse of ice reaching as far as the eye can see, broken only by low, jagged pressure ridges where the currents of the Arctic Ocean have doubled or tripled the ice thicknesses. Snow swirls in the hostile wind. Deep beneath the cap lies a world of valleys and mountains making up a terrain mapped in the past three decades by men who live in submarines. Undersea warriors now speak knowingly of Lomonosov Ridge, Makarov Basin, and Wrangel Plain much in the manner that tank drivers refer to the Fulda Gap.

On this short day, following a night of spectacular aurora borealis and bitter cold, the snout of a small seal at a tiny breathing hole breaks the white surface of the ice far above Wrangel Plain. The faintest of hisses accompanies a wisp of steam as it exhales. There is no other sound in the white expanse; even unheard is the soft padding of the white fox that follows a polar bear, the Lord of the Arctic.

A faint crackling a few milliseconds in length echoes off the underside of the ice pack. The seal is oblivious to it, as are the other denizens of the ice and ocean. But a large, sleek black shape beneath the ice has heard it, for the signal is man-made. The Akula submarine has been expecting this electronic signal from the huge Typhoon for which she is riding shotgun and maneuvers in a tight turn, her sensitive passive sonars searching for any trespassers. Satisfied at her privacy, the Akula moves off, separating herself from the Typhoon, and begins slowly patrolling in a wide circle about her charge as the huge submarine, a mountain of metal—a new Lord of the Arctic—commences the maneuvers for which she was designed.

The Typhoon probes the ice thickness with sonic beams, searching for the area of thinnest ice that is large enough to permit surfacing. Stolid and serious, the captain softly issues orders. Satisfied with the suitability of the frozen lead in the ice, he nods, and an officer passes an order on the announcing system, "Missile Stations!" Sailors and officers move quickly to their stations, hurdling the "knee-knockers," or thresholds, of the watertight doors.

The sub has twisted her great length with her twin propellers and has come to a dead stop, hovering with neutral buoyancy. Pumps move ballast water to sea, and the largest submarine in history rises slowly and almost gingerly below the four-foot-thick ice. The television camera shows little irregularity in the under-surface of the ice pack.

With a cannon-shot "crack," the massive sail and rudder break through, greeting a pale disc of sun on the horizon. Like a huge, wallowing whale, the rounded deck follows, gently lifting and rending the ice field.

The captain, now in heavy clothing and fur hat to protect him against the arctic winds, surveys the scene through the periscope. He receives missile-readiness reports, as well as reassurances from his electronic-sensor operators that there are no radar emissions and no sonar contacts. Only then does he climb up the long ladder to the Bridge. A sailor assists in pushing away a bit of ice, and the captain is finally able to search the horizon with his binoculars.

Sailors scramble topside, their exhalations forming a fog curtain about the ship as they struggle to clear away the large blocks of ice. Finally, the herculean efforts of this band of men (who never really "signed on" for this type of duty) permits the Typhoon to open her missile hatches—first one ... then another ... finally all twenty.

Satisfied with the demonstrated readiness of his crew and the Typhoon's missile battery, the captain issues a few soft orders, and the missile hatches slowly clang shut. He lights up a favorite pipe for a few luxurious puffs, gazes a final time at the peaceful scene, and lays below. Moments later, the Typhoon sinks slowly beneath the ice.

Typhoon's blackness contrasts starkly with the peaceful white Arctic, but she herself is a contradiction, a warship intended to prevent war—designed to fight a Cold War by not fighting at all.

But now that the Cold War has ended, what of Typhoon's mission? The nation-state that spawned Typhoon, the Soviet Union, is no more, and in its place is a confederation of independent republics, their exact definition and structure, and the roles of their navies, yet to be determined. In some cases trained men stand down and contemplate an uncertain future. Are the trips to the ice pack and the drills of opening muzzle doors to become memories?

And what of the magnificent Trident, or of those other marvels, the *Los Angeles*-class attack submarines? In a seeming frenzy, politicians in the United States view sharp reductions in military expenditures with great expectations, and the submarine force will not be exempt from the slashing of the military budget.

One has to examine the things that can be observed before cheering loudly. Despite the standing down of some ships, the dismantling of others, the talk of force reductions, of reciprocal exercises and visits, there is still and likely to remain for much time a distrust between nations and factions. Tridents and Typhoons still patrol.

A February 1992 issue of Izvestia quotes the captain of a

Typhoon submarine: "No one has changed my punched tapes yet. I don't know where my missiles are targeted. That kind of information is held only by the General Staff where the programs are written. But I have a good idea that the targets are military installations in one of the countries currently giving us humanitarian aid."

The breakout of peace is a cherished event. It appears, however, if history provides any lesson, that it is never permanent. Perhaps nations or sects are somehow preordained to have conflict. Some people even thrive on it. In fact, in recent years, when military leaders would have been happy to reduce the nuclear stockpiles, politicians saw it as a weakness in their administration should the levels of nuclear weapons fall "on their watch." Many of them, and their staffs, still labor to define damage radii and the like, viewing the use of nuclear weapons as a viable option in war, or as something with which they can exert a bully's club. But none of the politicians knows firsthand the power of nuclear weapons. It might be good to adopt a suggestion posed by James Schlesinger, a brilliant former Secretary of Defense—one who had a better feel for the effects of nuclear weapons than most: "Once every five years we should gather all the top leaders of all countries here in the desert to observe just a *small yield,* tens of kilotons, atmospheric test—make 'em stand here on top of the dune, not inside the blockhouse—in their underwear!" It would be a sobering learning experience.

Nevertheless, the submarines of the world's navies have helped to prevent a hot war. The Cold War has been expensive, but cheap compared to the alternative.

Those who would ask, "What now?" for the navies of the world, and especially for the submarine forces, need to take a long-term perspective. There is much hope for peace, kindled by the contacts between erstwhile adversaries and a greater openness among leaders. History records that strong alliances have grown between former bitter enemies—the United States and the United Kingdom, England and France, the Allies and Germany. Without doubt, there is room on Earth for more and closer friendships, but one should not expect miracles overnight, or even within the time span of several years.

Not long ago, in the late afternoon of a lovely autumn day in Hawaii, veterans congregated to mark the anniversary of the December 1941 attack on Pearl Harbor. That evening a retired U.S. Navy admiral was invited to visit a smart, beautiful, marvelously clean and polished submarine. The boat was impres-sive in every respect. She had enjoyed several weeks of inten-sive training under the supervision and guidance of experi-enced U.S. submariners, and the relationship of her crew with that of the nuclear sub assigned as her sponsor was marked by camaraderie.

This small diesel boat had earlier paid respects to the *Arizona* Memorial upon entering Pearl Harbor. That evening, her crew members would express respect for their American friends in another way. As the American ships throughout Pearl Harbor observed the sunset ceremony of lowering Old Glory, the visiting submarine also lowered her colors, the Rising Sun of the national ensign of Japan.

Fifty years in the making, but it can work.

◀

The "gold at the end of the rainbow" seen here is Polaris sub *George Washington Carver* returning to base at Holy Loch, Scotland, following a patrol in the North Atlantic. Rainsqualls, characteristic of the area, greet the boat's arrival as she passes Scottish villages. U.S. subs withdrew from this Scottish base after more than thirty years of effective use.

▲

A sonar operator in USS *John C. Calhoun* listens and watches the visual indications, apparently straining to pick out an elusive target from the sounds of whales, fish, shrimp, and extraneous shipping.

▲

The photo was taken at the moment the main ballast tank vents were opened to begin the diving sequence. Air spilling from the tanks forms geysers of spray as *Will Rogers* bids farewell to the normal earth's atmosphere for fifty-eight days of patrol.

At the Trident base in Kings Bay, Georgia, the SSBN tender *Canopus* tends older Polaris submarines. Seen here in the evening sunset, USS *Stimson* has just returned from patrol. ▶

(Inset) Because the range of the initial submarine-launched ballistic missiles was relatively short, only about 1,500 miles, the submarines had to be forward-based to be near their target areas. The first such base was established in Holy Loch, Scotland. USS *Proteus*, shown here, set up shop in Scotland in March 1961 as the first tender for Polaris submarines. She is shown loading a ballistic missile into a tube of one of the submarines. To command the tender, the Navy picked Captain Richard Laning, who had previously served as the first skipper of the nuclear-powered submarine *Seawolf*. An extrovert and gifted salesman, Laning had a public-relations role in addition to his operational mission. He had to sell the Scots on the idea that this new American presence was not harmful; indeed, it was helping to keep the peace between the Soviet Union and the western world. The initial deployments of the Polaris submarines from Holy Loch were under the leadership of Captain N. G. "Bub" Ward, ComSubRon 14, embarked in *Proteus*. He recalled later that he had a difficult time writing fitness reports on the skippers reporting to him. All were outstanding, so it was tough to differentiate among them; several later made flag rank. *(National Archives, 428-KN-1844)* ▶

During shakedown exercises following maintenance, the crew of *Will Rogers* enjoys a rare moment of strolling and relaxing topside in the calm Atlantic waters off Bermuda. ▶

During a Polaris patrol, Sunday church services in the crew's mess hall provide a break in the routine. The chief of the boat of USS *Will Rogers*, a volunteer lay leader, rigs the altar and outlines his sermon for the morning's church service. ▼

Despite raw wind and rain, dependents of USS *Georgia*'s crew flock to the Hood Canal floating bridge to wave a final goodbye to the departing Trident sub. In two months they will return to wave a welcome home.

◀

Georgia leaves for a patrol in the Pacific. The pilot for the base handles tugs as the captain gives advice to the officer of the deck, who conns the sub out the Hood Canal in Washington.

At Kings Bay, Georgia, missile technicians work on the missile tubes of *Casimir Pulaski* before off-loading missiles between patrols. ▶

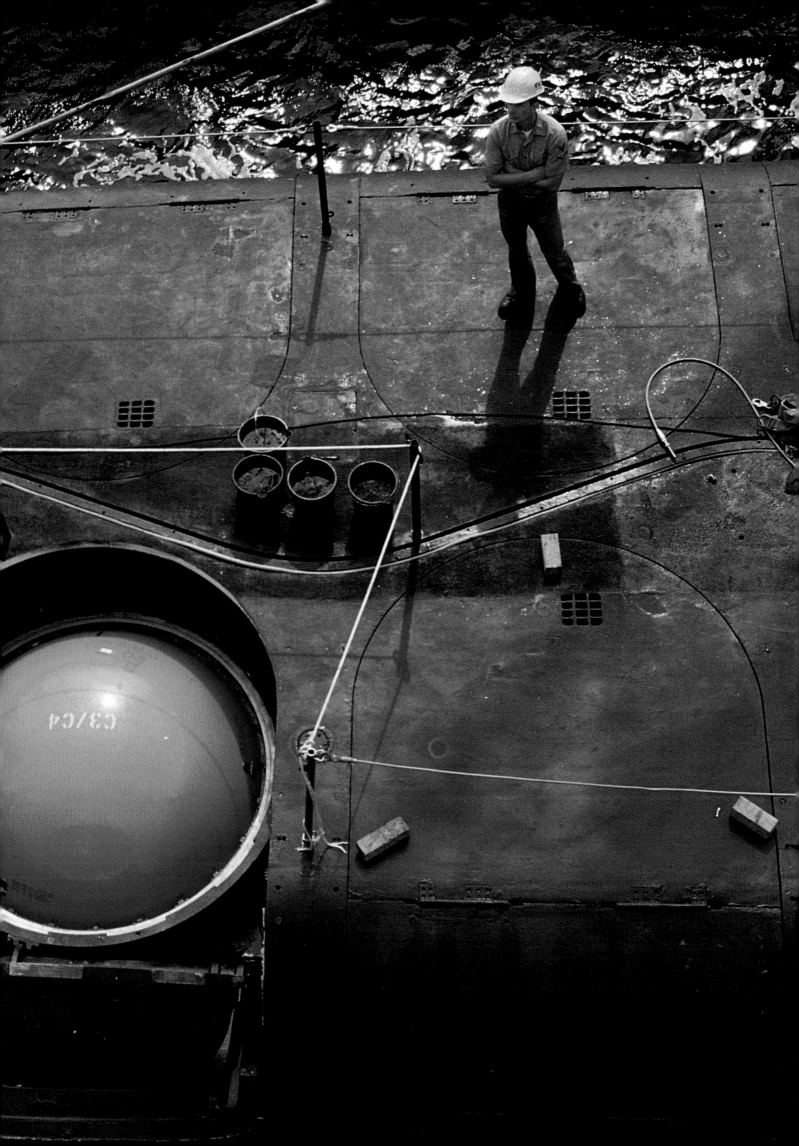

Perhaps no evolution is more demanding of skill, timing, and teamwork than the launch of Polaris or Poseidon missiles. The introduction of Trident has greatly improved the procedures. Seen here is a practice countdown of a full-load missile launch in the missile compartment of *John C. Calhoun.*

A Poseidon C-3 missile roars skyward upon breaking the surface, having been fired by *Ullysses S. Grant* during a demonstration and shakedown operation (DASO). ▶

The graving dock at the Trident base in Bangor, Washington, on the Hood Canal, is flooding to permit USS *Nevada* to float and leave after work on her bottom has been completed. With great sensitivity to ecological considerations, the dock was constructed as part of a delta-shaped pier, in 120 to 150 feet of water, to overcome the need for an additional pier, which would have obstructed the passage of salmon fingerlings. *Nevada* here is running her diesel engine to provide auxiliary electrical power because the reactor is not critical.

Nevada enters the explosive-handling wharf at Bangor to take on a load of missiles. Tugs assist the boat, countering the currents as line handlers pass lines to each wall of the wharf to hold the sub in place as she moves to the head of the wharf. The covered wharf provides safety as well as the capability to perform work in all weather.

In this bird's-eye view, *Nevada*'s line handlers, wearing life jackets in case they fall overboard into the cold water, look like spiders in a web. The men are skillfully working the lines to move the boat into missile-handling position at Bangor's explosive-handling wharf.

Inside a special facility at the Strategic Weapons Facility Pacific, Trident missile motors are examined by X-ray techniques developed by Lockheed.

A breathtaking vista shows USS *Georgia* moving into diving position in Dabob Bay, Washington, to commence post-repair trials. This sheltered bay, whose depth is in the hundreds of feet, provides an unusual capability for conducting submerged operations and noise trials within a very short distance of the base. ▶

◄◄
Submarine Base Bangor has been adjudged the finest and best-planned military base, rivaled now only by the Trident base at Kings Bay, Georgia. Here, in Washington's Hood Canal, may be seen the unique "delta" pier, which provides mooring for subs on two sides and dry-docking on the other side. To the north is the covered explosive-handling wharf.

◄◄
Full-scale missile tubes, cut away to facilitate an instructor's monitoring of students' actions, provide realistic training for missile technicians.

◄◄
At submarine bases, skilled divers fulfill a number of duties, ranging from doing underwater repairs to protecting against sabotage. Bangor-based divers dive on USS *Alabama* to repair an underwater fitting.

◄ At Submarine Base Bangor, the Trident Training Facility provides hands-on training with actual equipment installed in a boat's missile-control center.

For a number of years active protests were held at the gates of the Bangor base, usually peaceful in nature. Colorful balloons and costumes were featured in the roadblocks placed on the railroad tracks carrying missile motors to the base. ▼

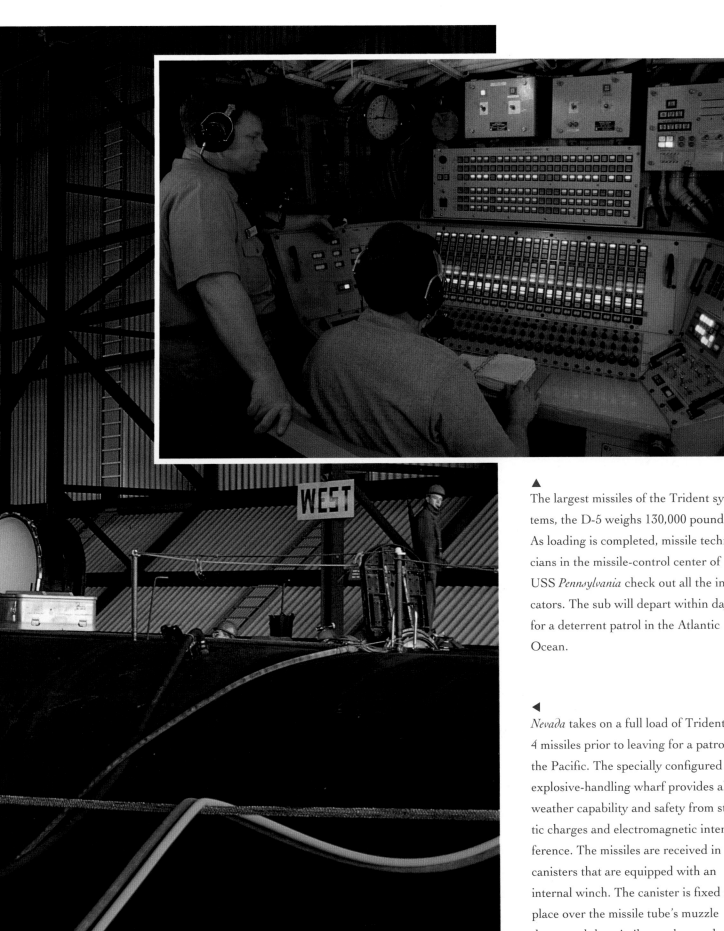

▲

The largest missiles of the Trident systems, the D-5 weighs 130,000 pounds. As loading is completed, missile technicians in the missile-control center of USS *Pennsylvania* check out all the indicators. The sub will depart within days for a deterrent patrol in the Atlantic Ocean.

◄

Nevada takes on a full load of Trident C-4 missiles prior to leaving for a patrol in the Pacific. The specially configured explosive-handling wharf provides all-weather capability and safety from static charges and electromagnetic interference. The missiles are received in canisters that are equipped with an internal winch. The canister is fixed in place over the missile tube's muzzle doors, and the missiles are lowered or raised within the canisters, thus freeing the crew from problems that would otherwise arise from boat movement due to waves.

Submarine Base Kings Bay is the base for subs equipped
with the largest submarine missiles, the 130,000-pound D-5,
which fully fills the large tubes of the Trident submarines.
Through nation-to-nation agreements, the U.S. extends support of the D-5 to the submarines of the United Kingdom.
Under the protection of a covered explosive-handling wharf,
Pennsylvania carries out the high-security loading operation
prior to departing on patrol.

Within the covered explosive-handling wharf, *Nevada* opens the muzzle hatches of all her missile tubes and makes final preparations and adjustments inside before receiving a loadout of Trident missiles. At the bottom of the tubes, missile technicians precisely set the rings on which the missiles will rest.

◄

(Inset) The transportation of missiles from the strategic-weapons facility to a submarine at the explosive-handling wharf is rigidly controlled. Each missile is convoyed with heavily armed U.S. Marine Corps escorts, who also patrol and maintain security within the entire facility.

◄

Strategic Weapons Facility Pacific, a stowage and assembly facility for Trident weapons, is a "super-security" facility, heavily alarmed and guarded by three hundred marines.

Protected by armed escorts, the Trident submarine *Nevada* transits the muddy Panama Canal en route to the Pacific Ocean. The crew on deck includes the captain, who is taking photos of the scene. There are two situations in which the commanding officer relinquishes his responsibility for his boat, after a pilot assumes charge when transiting the Panama Canal, and from entering a dry dock until departing the dry dock, during which time the ship is the responsibility of the docking officer. The crew here enjoys a rare sunbath and barbecue, traditional for missile boats making the canal transit.

As USS *Nevada* is lowered through the last stage of the Panama Canal, the Miraflores Lock, a deluge pours two inches of rain onto the deck in fifteen minutes, chasing sightseers below. ▼

◀

Michigan's crew maintains fitness on patrol by working out on exercise equipment or by running in the missile compartment. Runners do a marathon at the peril of knees and elbows, rounding sharp corners to complete a circuit in which nineteen laps are required for a mile.

An Engineering Laboratory technician, a specialist in radiation safety, monitors radiation at the boundary between the reactor compartment and the missile compartment of USS *Michigan.* ▼

◀

In USS *Michigan,* the crew conducts a casualty drill—repairing a major steam leak. The protective suit permits working in very hot spaces with live steam.

As USS *Ohio*, a Trident submarine based in Bangor, Washington, returns home through the Hood Canal, one of the crew is fitted out in a wet suit and serves as a lifeguard for anyone who should have the misfortune to fall overboard. Mod sun glasses on the sailor reflect the Hood Canal floating bridge through which *Ohio* will shortly pass. ▶

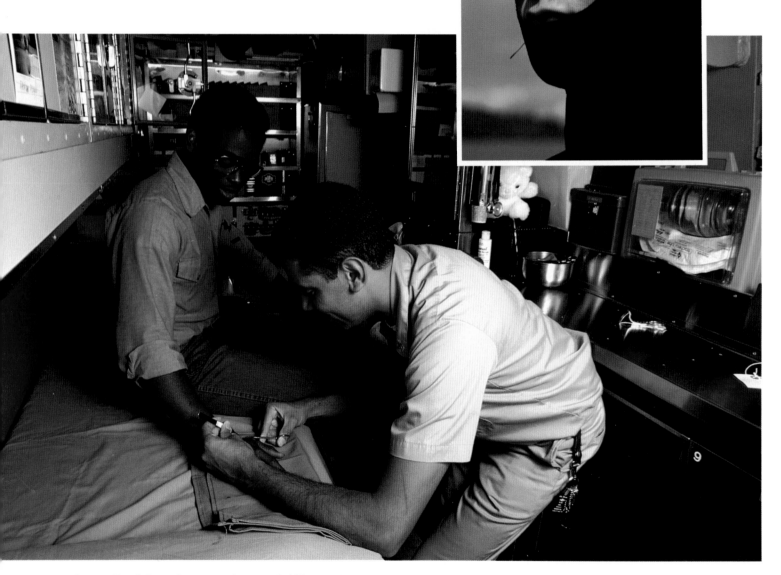

In the small sick bay of USS *Michigan,* a chief hospitalman removes stitches from a wound and checks the condition of a crew member. For years nuclear subs carried doctors, but as the need proved unfounded, they were transferred to hospitals and dispensaries, where the need for their services was greater. Hospitalmen qualified for independent duty provide health care and valued guidance to skippers.

Radiomen of ballistic-missile submarines know that their task is to assure that, as nearly as possible, the boat maintains 100-percent reception capability for messages from the National Command Authority. Redundant transmissions from the powerful very low frequency and extremely low frequency stations assure reception while the sub is deep and avoid the necessity for exposing antennas, which could lead to detection of the submarine and decreased credibility of the deterrent. ▶

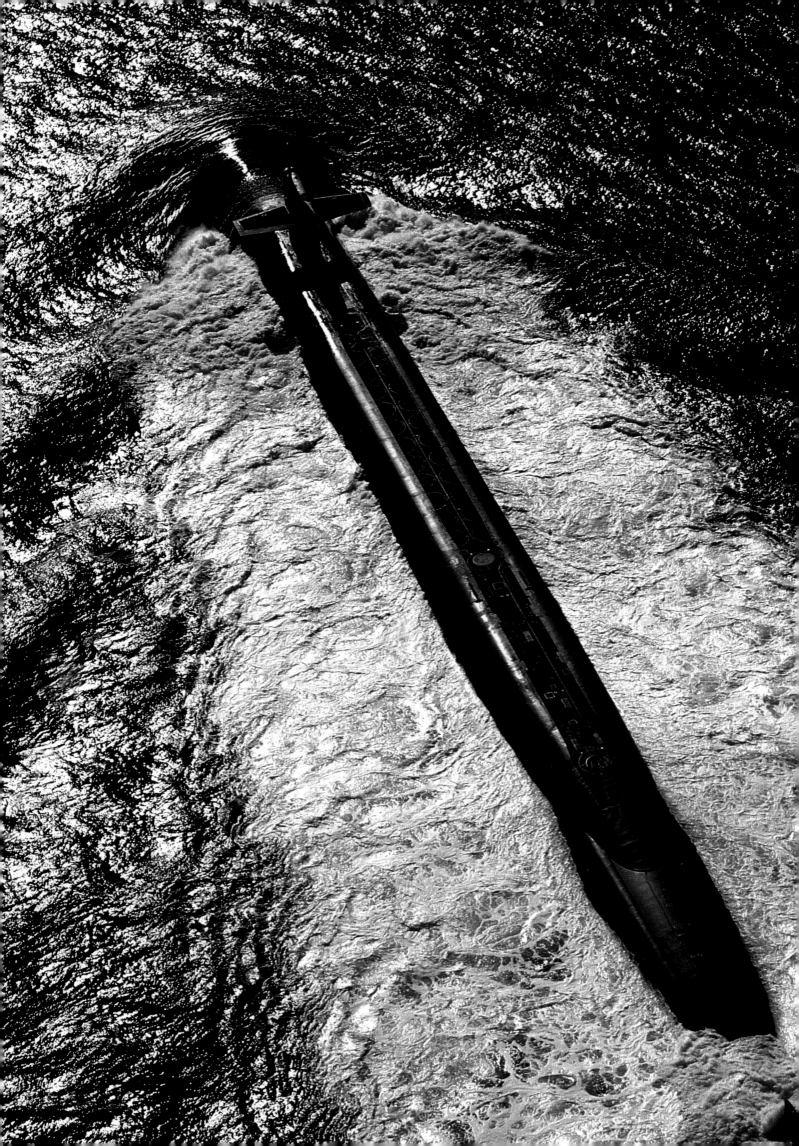

The Trident sub *Georgia* runs at high speed in the Straits of Juan de Fuca between the United States and Canada, headed for her diving point to begin a patrol in the Pacific Ocean.

The captain of USS *Georgia* supervises the maneuvers of his large Trident sub going through post-maintenance testing in the confined waters of Dabob Bay, Washington. Standing at the elevated periscope station in the sub's Control Room, he can readily oversee the conduct of those controlling the course and depth of his submerged boat. ▶

▲

The Trident submarine *Georgia*, longer than the Washington Monument and almost twice the tonnage of World War II cruisers, appears almost spritely as she leaps from 300 feet to the surface in Dabob Bay, Washington. This maneuver is not normal, but a special test to ensure the proper operation of high-pressure air valves, which can admit air under great pressure into the main ballast tanks in the event the sub encounters serious flooding from the rupture of large circulating-water piping or from a submerged collision.

Family grams are a great morale builder for deployed submarine crews. Limited to fifty words, dependents are able to pass on to deployed husbands vital news to bridge the gap in communications, a most welcome message even if it is only one-way. Seen here are the wife and son of a USS *Ohio* chief petty officer, depositing a family gram in the "mailbox" at the Bangor, Washington, base.

▲

Dawn finds USS *Georgia,* a large Trident sub, starting post-upkeep sea trials in sheltered Dabob Bay. The Olympic Mountains provide a scenic backdrop through the layers of morning mist and fog.

◄

A young woman watches as USS *Michigan* heads out the Hood Canal with her new husband aboard.

The largest of the world's submarines, a Russian Typhoon shows great positive buoyancy, looming as a mountain over the pier at Severomorsk, Russia.　▶

On top of the Bridge of the Typhoon submarine that he commands, Captain (First Rank) Andrej Zhygilev relaxes in the port of Severomorsk, Russia, prior to getting under way. ▶

View of the massive Typhoon from the bow gives a feeling of its great size and length–like Tridents, almost two football fields long. The cleats and heavy mooring lines that tie the sub to the pier will be stowed in lockers as the ship goes to sea. ▶▶

On a beautiful clear night during the annual Navy Day celebration several Russian submarine school sailors watch a colorful fireworks display, enjoyed by thousands ashore, while bobbing gently on a motor launch in the Neva River at St. Petersburg. ▶▶▶

Very impressive bulbous sail and fairwater of the Typhoon loom high over the main deck of the world's largest submersible. ▼

The topside watch of the Japanese sub *Akishio*
(SS-579) lowers the colors, the "Rising Sun" flag,
at sunset alongside the pier in Pearl Harbor,
Hawaii, in concert with U.S. submarines.

THE NAVAL INSTITUTE PRESS

Sharks of Steel

Designed by Pamela Lewis Schnitter

Set in Bembo and Cochin in Adobe Post Script on a
Macintosh IIci and output by Artech Graphics II, Inc.,
Baltimore, Maryland

Printed on 80-lb Lithofect Gloss
by J. D. Lucas in Baltimore, Maryland and
bound in James River Iris with Rainbow Parchment
endsheets